## True Tales of the Strange and Supernatural



MICHAEL D. WYNNE

PELICAN PUBLISHING
New Orleans

ISBN 9781455628056

*Cover and interior photographs by Michael D. Wynne*

Printed in the United States of America
Published by Pelican Publishing
New Orleans, LA
www.pelicanpub.com

*Dedicated to my beloved "scary" grandchildren*

*Emma Grace Wynne,*

*Ewan Alexander Watt,*

*Crosby Michael Wynne,*

*Everett Murray Watt,*

*and Elliott Watt*

# CONTENTS

# Acknowledgments

There are so many good and gracious people who have directly contributed to this book that I am eternally grateful to.

Regarding Hotel Bentley and Diamond Grill Restaurant, I am indebted to Mike Jenkins, Scott Laliberte, Martha Turner, Felicia McCloud, and Beulah Davis. Mike is the beloved owner of the "Bentley" (as locals call it), the Diamond Grill, Loyd Hall, and so many other historic and important properties. Without Mike Jenkins, the quality and standard of living in Central Louisiana would be much, much lower. Scott is the President and Chief Operating Officer of Mike's properties, and Martha is the manager of the Bentley. Both are well-respected leaders in the business community. Felicia has helped me so much with facilitating my interviews and site visits. Beulah is a living legend full of stories on Loyd Hall.

Regarding Myrtle Groves Huie-Dellmon House, I am indebted to Celise Reech Harper, director of the Rapides Parish Library, Wes Saunders, and Beth Vandersteen, retired director of the West Baton Rouge Parish Library. All are extraordinary public servants and good friends.

Regarding Kent House, I am indebted to Alice Scarborough, the executive director of the Kent House, tour guide LeAnn Raines, and the board of directors of Kent House. I have had the pleasure of working with them for more than two decades, and there are no better people in the state in similar positions.

Regarding James W. Bolton House, I am indebted Sudha and Amarjit "Amy" Pillarisetti, current owners of the historic Bolton House. Both are important leaders in the Central Louisiana community and longtime friends.

Regarding Tyrone Plantation, I am indebted to Judge F. Rae Swent, owner of Tyrone. Friends for nearly forty years, Rae is one of the true leaders of historic preservation in Louisiana as well as a lovely lady.

Regarding the (Old) Rapides Cemetery, I am indebted to the City of Pineville, especially the Honorable Rich Dupree, Chief Doug Gann and the Pineville City Council, Tom David, as well as historian extraordinaire Paul Price. The City of Pineville owns the (Old) Rapides Cemetery and should be thanked for their dedication to the cemetery's preservation. Paul, a friend for many years, is the essence of a historian and preservation. He doesn't just talk history and preservation; he does something about it.

Regarding the "Unknown Civil War Soldier," I am indebted the Knights of Columbus, Third Degree Bishop Greco Council #1134 and the Knights of Columbus, Monsignor Piegard Fourth Degree Council, and especially to Donald "Donnie" Bolton, Phil Chatelain, Wayne Alford, Al Mathews, David Fett, Leonard Wilson, Carl Berlin, Ronald "Ronnie" Mayeaux, Chris Cancienne, David Lacaze, Gene Alford, James Marien, Scott Speir, Pat Kelly, Earl Basco, Danny Bordelon, Alan Daenen, Jeremiah Johnson, Al Bedoya, and others. Additionally, I am indebted to Father Anthony "Raj" Dharmaraj, and Father Tom Kennedy, Dr. Chip McGimsey, Graham Kramer and his staff at Kramer Funeral Homes and Greenwood Memorials. The soldier's interment was an act of love and a team effort.

Regarding Old Pineville City Hall, I am indebted again to the City of Pineville, especially the Honorable Rich Dupree, Chief Doug Gann, and the Pineville City Council. This important building is being saved by all of them.

Regarding Walnut Grove Plantation, I am indebted to Dr. Jill LeBlanc Larson and Paul Larson for the kindness extended to me. Cheryl McGowen was of great assistance in alerting me to his historic (and ghostly) property.

Regarding Mimi's Ghostbuster's, I am indebted to "Mimi," also known as Brenda Frick, and team members Tracy Bryant, Margaret Bryant, Gwen Ruppert, Fane Ruppert, Brandt Ruppert, and Madylin Fritsche, as well as the rest of the remarkable team that makes up "Mimi's Ghostbusters." I admire all of them for what they are doing. The other ghost investigators, Louisiana Spirits Paranormal Investigators, is a fabulous group and has done groundbreaking work in this field.

Regarding support and guidance, I am truly indebted to my dear friend Cheré Dastugue Coen who suggested that I write this book and contacted Pelican Publishing on my behalf to make it happen. Scott Campbell, the publisher at Pelican Publishing, and editor Justin Mason are wonderful professionals to work with.

I am indebted to the publishers of my various monthly magazine articles including: Will Harp Jr. of *Cenla Focus* magazine, Juanita Vanderlick of *Visible Horizons*, Orkke Clifton of *318 Central* magazine, Abigail Blalock of *Pineville Living* magazine and Alaina Nunnally of *Alexandria Living* magazine.

I am indebted to many supportive friends including Paul Price and Mike Tudor, both of Pineville and premier historians, community leaders, and good friends. Others that I am indebted to include Katie Vanderlick and the Alexandria-Pineville Convention and Visitor's Bureau, Celise Reech Harper and staff at the Rapides Parish Library in Alexandria, Jojuana Phillips and the reporters and staff at KALB television station, Scott Owens of River Ridge, Jen Rodgers, Phillip Coco, Shirley Bell Rasberry, Sylvia Yancy Davis, Kristy Belgard, Melissa Scarborough, and Jan Wilson Farmer.

My mentors include Leon Bergeron Jr., my neighbor, Robin Miller, writer extraordinaire, Dr. Henry Robertson, historian extraordinaire, Pierre E. Conner, and of course, the greatest of them all, the late historian and writer Lyle Saxon. I'm sure I missed somebody important to list and if I did, I sincerely apologize to you.

And last and most importantly not least, I am indebted to my family for putting up with me and all this work.

# Introduction

According to the book *Gumbo Ya-Ya,* there are many beliefs and stories exclusive to Louisiana concerning the supernatural, including these beliefs:

Spirits sometimes make their appearance in the form of a cat or a rabbit. You can tell spirit-cats and spirit-rabbits from ordinary cats and rabbits by the fact that the former can disappear at will.

Sometimes, when the wind is blowing, or there is a small whirlwind, horses in a pasture will break and run. They do so because they have seen a spirit, presumably in the wind.

Jack-o'-lanterns (swamp lights) are said to lead searchers to buried treasure. They are very mischievous and delight to harass animals, particularly horses, whom they cause to shy, or to resist the rider's directions. They also follow hunting parties, misleading dogs. They are usually unseen by humans. . . .

The spirits of people who were associated in life are to be found together, and all keep their original characteristics. Sometimes lying spirits amuse themselves by giving false clues. Spirits haunt the places they frequented in life, and when they are not in the form of a cat or a rabbit, they may be seen in a vaporous form resembling their former body. If such a vapor strikes a solid object, it disappears like a burst bubble. Usually, spirits do no harm but merely gather in their former home at night where they may be seen talking until

> dawn. Sometimes they will appear to a former friend and direct him to some long-lost possession, though often the recipient of the message is so disturbed that the message must be repeated on successive occasions. . . .
>
> Vindictive spirits are usually those of murdered men. These never cease to plague or question their murderers. On almost every plantation there was someone who was witch-ridden. Such a one would have terrible spasms, screaming and grabbing about. The only way to give the sufferer relief was to take hold of him, but this was only temporary, for as soon as he again fell asleep, the witches would return. . . .

According to the book *Louisiana: A Guide to the State,* here are some of the ways to prevent ghosts from inhabiting your home:

> If you are troubled with ghosts, hang a horseshoe on your front or back door, burn sawdust and sprinkle the ashes in the corners of the house, burn two white candles on the floor in front of your fireplace, turn your pockets inside out, and never pass a cemetery unless you are holding a little child by the hand. If you are still bothered, confront the ghosts and tell them you are angry and perhaps they will go away. Otherwise, turn around three times and spit on them. If you are afraid of a dead person, pin two new straight pins in the form of a cross on the corpse or place a bottle of white chicken feathers on the grave, and, unless his *gris gris* is stronger than yours, he won't haunt you. . . .

In considering the realm of spirituality, the two big questions that everyone should be asking themselves are:

What are ghosts (or spirits)?

Do I personally believe in ghosts and spirits?

Well, only *you* can answer the second question, a question that even I have personally wrestled with for some time, with no final decision yet made. Whether or not there are ghosts or spirits, by all the accounts in this book, there is definitely something happening, something unexplainable, something mysterious, something fascinating, and something almost unbelievable.

As to the first question, *What are ghosts (or spirits)?* there are many and varied definitions. One good and short definition is:

> "An apparition of a dead person which is believed to appear or become manifest to the living, typically as a nebulous image."

Wikipedia's definition is much more expanded; here is the essence of that definition:

> In folklore, a ghost is the soul or spirit of a dead person or non-human animal that is believed to be able to appear to the living. In ghost lore, descriptions of ghosts vary widely, from an invisible presence to translucent or barely visible wispy shapes to realistic, lifelike forms. The deliberate attempt to contact the spirit of a deceased person is known as necromancy, or in spiritism as in séance. Other terms associated with it are apparition, haunt, phantom, poltergeist, shade, specter, spirit, spook, wraith, demon, and ghoul.
>
> The belief in the existence of an afterlife, as well as manifestations of the spirits of the dead, is widespread, dating back to animism or ancestor worship in pre-literate cultures. Certain religious practices—funeral rites, exorcisms, and some practices of spiritualism and ritual magic—are specifically designed to rest the spirits of the dead. Ghosts are generally described as solitary, human-like essences, though stories of ghostly armies and the ghosts of animals other than humans have also been recounted. They are believed to haunt particular locations, objects, or people they were associated with in life. According to a 2009 study by the Pew Research Center, 18 percent of Americans say they have seen a ghost.
>
> The overwhelming consensus of science is that there is no proof that ghosts exist. Their existence is impossible to falsify, and ghost hunting has been classified as a pseudoscience. Despite centuries of investigation, there is no scientific evidence that any location is inhabited by the spirits of the dead. Historically, certain toxic and psychoactive plants (such as *Datura* and *Hyoscyamus niger*), whose use has long been associated with necromancy and the underworld, have been shown to contain anticholinergic compounds that are pharmacologically linked to dementia (specifically DLB) as well as histological patterns of neurodegeneration. Recent research has indicated that ghost sightings may be related to degenerative brain diseases such as Alzheimer's disease. Common prescription medication and over-the-counter drugs (such as sleep aids) may also, in rare instances, cause ghost-like hallucinations, particularly

> zolpidem and diphenhydramine. Older reports linked carbon monoxide poisoning to ghost-like hallucinations. . . .

In writing and assembling this book, I am acting in the guise of a reporter; I am reporting what others are saying. This is not a scientific study nor a documentary. Some may even consider this book a book of horror stories, of entertainment, or even just a travel guide for those who want to personally visit and engage in spiritual places. This book should mostly be considered a thoughtful telling of many reliable (and a few less reliable) stories that tell of sightings of spooks, ghosts, apparitions and of the evidence of the spiritual world. The reader should decide on their own as to what is true and what is not. I will not past judgment on the testimony heretofore provided, nor will I support and try to boost the testimony either. I fully respect the reader's own judgment to make their own decision as to the viability of the spiritual world here in Central Louisiana.

This book concentrates on the spiritual world in Central Louisiana. Outside of New Orleans, there is no more active spirited place in all of Louisiana. The book first addresses the Alexandria and Pineville area locations, the most urban cities in Central Louisiana, then moves on to the rest of Rapides Parish, the most central and urban locale here in Central Louisiana. This book then addresses the other parishes using a broad definition of Central Louisiana. Last, the book addresses Bigfoot, not as much a spirit as a creature, and the book ends with a beloved haunted tale from a master storyteller.

I have seriously endeavored to be inclusive and list all the reported spirited locations in Central Louisiana, but I probably missed many. This book is a first of its kind in Central Louisiana so I had no previous good source to focus on as a primary reference; I had to find most of these sites on my own.

I ask the reader only to do one thing and one thing only: put aside your preconceived notions on the spirit world and open your heart and mind. Read what others, people just like you, have to say about what they have seen, heard, and experienced. And always remember that there are more mysteries out there in this wondrous world that we cannot understand than those that we can understand.

# Alexandria's Spirited Sites

# Hotel Bentley

## "While You Sleep, They Roam"

Ghost hunting shows are popular and fascinating among the many enthusiasts of those shows. People are simply fascinated with not only the spirit world but also with those who hunt for the spirit world. The interest in ghost hunters clearly goes back hundreds of years, back to our innate desire to solve crimes and mysteries and the creation of the crime/murder detective. We just don't want to see the spirit world exposed; we want to be part of the satisfaction of exposing this world ourselves. The joy comes from the proverbial "thrill of the chase." Ghost hunters have tapped into this thrill, this want of being part of something exciting. The journey to the destination in this case is often better than the arrival to the scene.

In December of 2010, ghost hunters arrived in Alexandria. Their shiny black SUVs pulled into downtown Alexandria so prominently that the then-Alexandria chief of police himself, Chief Roger Tully, escorted them into an area surrounded by barricades. They were special guests in a city filled with ghost sightings, several that this team of hunters would be hunting for evidence for.

Robert K. Ripley of *Ripley's Believe It or Not* declared Alexandria as a "ghost city" way back in 1930. Back then, Ripley called Alexandria this name as there were no cemeteries within the city limits of Alexandria, then a city of 23,010 in population. Of course, the explanation was that Alexandria was of a lower sea level than that of its brother city Pineville located just across the Red River. The deceased were ferried from Alexandria to Pineville and were buried in one of the many cemeteries that dot the downtown Pineville landscape, making the City of Pineville to one day designate downtown Pineville as the state's only "cemetery district."

The "ghost hunters" who came to Alexandria were members of a team from the television SyFy program *Ghost Hunters*. Jason Hawes and Grant Wilson, leaders of The Atlantic Paranormal Society (TAPS), are the stars of the program. According to the *Ghost Hunters* website, "Contact between humans and the spirits from the afterlife is not as farfetched as it seems. As plumbers by day and ghost hunters by night, Jason Hawes, Grant Wilson, and their team have worked to track down the presence of paranormals across the country."

Reportedly, not only were there certain buildings in Alexandria that had ghosts and spirits, but also in at least one case, one spirit was floating from building to building downtown.

The *Ghost Hunters* crew pulled up to the Hotel Bentley, the Diamond Grill restaurant, and to Finnegan's Wake pub, all of which are located along Third Street. On each of the crews' vehicles were stickers with TAPS in big, bold letters placed on the front, sides, and rear of the vehicles.

TAPS is an organization that investigates reported paranormal activity. Based in Warwick, Rhode Island, TAPS was founded in 1995 by Jason Hawes and Grant Wilson. In 2004, the organization itself became the subject of *Ghost Hunters*. The show ran for eleven seasons on SyFy in the US.

It all started in 1990 when Hawes began the Rhode Island Paranormal Society (RIPS), after having a personal experience with spirits. After RIPS began investigating cases throughout the New England area, Jason met up with Grant Wilson in 1995 and they formed TAPS together. Wilson had also had a personal experience. Neither man talks about their experiences in public. The group was originally run out of Jason's basement, and at that time the team consisted only of Jason and Grant. They pioneered investigative techniques that many other paranormal investigators now use. In 2003, they were approached by Pilgrim Films and taped ten episodes of *Ghost Hunters* for the SyFy channel.

TAPS traditionally sends a group of three to eight members to perform an eight- to sixteen-hour investigation, covering multiple nights, employing a number of infrared and digital video cameras, thermal camera devices, EMF (electromagnetic field) detectors, digital thermometers, and other equipment throughout the site in question. While at a site, the members of the team often find common explanations for the claims of the occupants. In conclusion, the team will report on its findings and express their opinion that a site is "haunted" or "not haunted." The group distinguishes themselves from other paranormal groups by going into a case by claiming they wish to *disprove* a haunting rather than *prove* a haunting. TAPS does not charge their clients for the investigations or for consultation.

Regarding the history of the grand old Hotel Bentley, legend has it that Joseph Andrew Bentley (1860-1938) built the hotel in 1907 because he was denied a room at another hotel because his clothes were dirty after a day of hard work logging timber. The storied and beloved hotel opened on August 10, 1908. Bentley lived in the hotel in his second-floor apartment until his death at age seventy-seven in June 1938.

Bentley is buried in his native Pennsylvania, in Williamsport, but many say he never left the hotel. Several staff at the hotel have seen his ghost through the years.

This grand hotel building, located at 801 Third Street in Alexandria, was built from clay and limestone from the nearby Red River. Bentley owned a generator that powered his apartment and that of the famed "Mirror Room," the main entertainment room for the hotel. The rest of the hotel did not have air-conditioning in its early years. Instead, the windows could be opened, and when the wind would come off the river, the guests could feel the breeze. Bentley never married and many say he considered the hotel as his "wife."

In 1938, architect George Mann added an additional three stories to the Bentley (as it is often called by local people) with the hotel then totaling eighty rooms and eight stories. In 1960, the Bentley closed for nearly a decade. But in the 1980s, Robert B. "Buddy" Tudor Jr. (1935-2010), bought it and remodeled the aging landmark. It reopened and stayed open for fifteen years. After changing hands a couple times, it was sold to Bob Dean. Bob Dean owned many nursing homes and at one time considered turning the hotel into a nursing home itself. But the city of Alexandria turned down his proposal. Then he considered tearing down the Bentley and was again denied. Michael "Mike" Jenkins now owns the hotel and not only saved it from destruction; he had it fully restored and refurbished in 2012. The hotel now consists of approximately 92-94 rooms. Celebrities from all walks of life have stayed at the Bentley including, but not limited to John Wayne, Roy Rodgers, Omar Bradley as well as infamous Louisiana governors, Huey Long, and Earl Long.

Hawes and Nolan and the production company, Pilgrim Films and Television, would film at the Hotel Bentley and in downtown Alexandria for

*The Hotel Bentley*

sixteen days. This show premiered on television on February 23, 2011, and was seen by nine million viewers and continues to be seen today over the internet. The video of the ghost hunters shows the investigators taking data and exploring the Hotel Bentley extensively. It is obvious from watching the video and the conversations between investigators that many spirits haunt this cherished old hotel. The video is well worth watching. As was ultimately reported by *Ghostbusters,* "The historic Hotel Bentley . . . was portrayed as a veritable hotbed of ghosts." You must watch the video to get the full impact of what the team discovered.

This was not only the only ghost hunting-type team to visit the Hotel Bentley. The Louisiana Spirits Paranormal (LSP) investigators also came for an investigative tour in 2020.

The LSP group is very similar to the TAPS group, but by definition, the LSP group is a statewide group that almost entirely visits only Louisiana locations.

According to the *Town Talk*, a four-person team from LSP, investigators were given access to the hotel on Halloween 2020 according to Grady Welch, then case manager for the Central Louisiana chapter of the organization. Part of their report noted the experiences that prior guests of the hotel have had:

> The smell of smoke from a pipe or a cigar where people who do not smoke. (I reported this matter and) Called down to the front desk and told them they haven't been smoking (and please) do not charge the $250 smoking fee. (Also) People coming into the rooms or walking in their rooms (have said):

> "I stayed in the bridal suite upstairs. Upon entering the room, I placed my cell phone on the table. It flew across the room onto the floor. Then it kept turning the Jacuzzi on and off. I could feel that the place is so haunted."
>
> —Brent J. Maia (August 22, 2019)

> "I worked at the hotel in the late 1990s. We all know that the (hotel) was inhabited with spirits. The (former) owner (Joseph Bentley) likes visiting the dining room. I would straighten the photos in the hallway going to the restroom and each time they would be put back crooked. I used to joke with him about it that he just like to play jokes. We would always (receive calls at) the front desk about someone coming into the room or someone walking down the hallway. I cannot remember which room. . . . When the customers tell us of these things, it didn't surprise us because we all knew. It was a wonderful place to work because there is so much history there. You could sometimes feel the spirit and see the people of the past."
>
> —Kathryn (August 1, 2017)

According to the LSP report from 2020, some of the other recent paranormal activities that have been reported also include:

> The staff elevator door started to close and then opened like someone was getting on and no one was there to get on.
>
> People reported someone walking up and down the hallway and coming out of rooms when no one was there.
>
> There were reports of sounds like someone was coming into occupied rooms late at night.

Their investigation unfolded this way. According to the LSP report, the LSP team arrived and investigated the Bentley beginning on October 31, 2020. The equipment used was a Mel meter, K2 meters, a night vision video camera, a UV digital still camera, SB7 spirit box, and digital voice recorders.

> We started our investigation off in the basement area near the laundry room. There are reports of a little girl that likes to play with the employees in this area. We captured a fast-moving anomaly that can be seen in the video evidence. We also captured some spikes on the Mel meter which was seen on the camera. We also got a

> response on one of our K2 meters to a direct question to the little girl. We also captured an unexplained screeching or screaming sound on audio. The second part of our investigation took place up on the sixth floor in the condo area, which is still under renovation and is not open to the public. We did receive some interesting spikes on the K2 meters, but unfortunately this was not captured on video. We did capture an interesting anomaly on video that can be seen in the evidence. It comes in from left side of frame and floats to center bottom, but twists and fades in and out.

The team had first started in the basement to see if they could detect the spirit of a seven-year-old little girl who reportedly died after falling down an elevator shaft. The child's ghost reportedly "likes to tug on people's clothing or touch them."

The LSP team's report concluded as follows:

> Louisiana Spirits has pioneered so many reportedly active locations in the state. By not simply going off haunted tales, we treat any historic location as the next potential haunting. In some cases, we walk out empty-handed, other times we don't. In regard to the Hotel Bentley, we strongly feel activity is prevalent here and we believe that with the help of a follow-up investigation, we will be able to get more evidence!

Grady Welch said then that the group definitely picked up on activity, even some voices and fluctuations on EMF detectors. He said then that he would love to go back and do some more research if allowed.

There is another documented report on spiritual sightings at the Bentley. This report (given in 2023 to the author) was from Jen Rodgers, then of the Alexandria-Pineville Convention and Visitor's Bureau. She said:

> It was in 1999 when I had worked there. It was then owned by Bob Dean and was part of the Radisson chain. I heard a story from one of the bellboys when he was taking up one of the patron's luggage. The hallway was empty. He said that he could hear footsteps directly behind him. He looked back and no one was there.
>
> Then being the curious person that I am, I went up to the fourth floor to see. I didn't believe in ghosts or spirits up until that time. I remember hearing footsteps behind me (when I arrived there). I was

> all alone. I had this eerie feeling. It wasn't a dangerous eerie feeling, just that a spirit was there other than my own. I left the scene very quickly. From then on, I always walked fast (at the Bentley) and tried not to be ever alone. Who knows what prominent person that it was. Was it Mr. Bentley himself?

According to research supplied by Roger Bell of the Jefferson Highway Association:

> **Is the Hotel Bentley Haunted?**
>
> Stories of ghosts in the hotel have regularly occurred. The hotel has been the site of multiple paranormal investigations and was featured in a 2011 *Ghost Hunters* episode of the television program.
>
> One spirit that has regularly (been) seen by guests over the years is that of a young girl who fell to her death when she tripped and fell into an open elevator shaft. She is sometimes seen by guests in random hallways or when stepping out of the elevator. The child ghost supposedly also likes to tug on people's clothing or touch them.
>
> The spirit of the builder of the hotel, Joseph Bentley, has also been spotted and is known to favor the fifth floor. Employees have also seen him from time to time in the Mirror Room area of the hotel.
>
> In 1946, a young man from Alabama had a tragic and fatal fall down the staircase of the hotel. An apparition matching his description has also been seen in areas of the hotel and especially late at night near the staircase area.

**Writer's Note:** Regarding this last incident—as reported in the Alexandria *Town Talk* on August 30, 1946, Carter Bell of Birmingham, Alabama, had just left the hotel bar and was walking up the marble steps along with three friends. He suddenly turned at the top of the steps purportedly to speak to his friends and fell down the hard steps to the mid-way landing. A coroner's jury was quickly assembled and determined that his fall was accidental, and Bell fractured his neck and head. Bell may have had a sudden cerebral hemorrhage at the top of the steps. All of this was witnessed by several men. Strangely, Bell's three friends who proceeded him up the steps were all medical doctors! The main lobby area witness who claimed to have witnessed the actual fall was also a doctor! What are the chances of four unrelated doctors being a witness to a single tragic death?! No documentation has yet been found regarding the death of the young girl down an elevator shaft.

The Hotel Bentley is one of the greatest treasures in Louisiana regarding historic buildings. Owner Michael Jenkins deserves full credit and adulation for the restoration and management of this masterpiece. Go stay there and make your own judgment, but be prepared to meet the ghostly permanent residents of the grand and extraordinary Hotel Bentley.

# Diamond Grill

## "Who Is Really There Serving Your Meal?"

The Diamond Grill, one of the important investigative stops for the TAPS team, occupies what was for many years Schnack's Fine Jewelry store. (See the prior chapter on the Hotel Bentley to learn more about what the TAPS team is all about.) The building was built around 1865 as a jewelry store by Scottish immigrants. It was later purchased by a German named Carl A Schnack (1849-1918). Schnack continued to keep the jewelry store open but renamed it as Schnack's Fine Jewelry. It quickly became a landmark for the city of Alexandria. In the 1990s, the store moved to another location, leaving the beautiful art deco-style building empty. Several years later after being unoccupied for some time, it was purchased by the grandson of the builder, Robert B. "Buddy" Tudor Jr. (1935-2010). Tudor turned the beautiful store into a fine dining restaurant. To pay homage to the jewelry store that was there beforehand, he decided to call the restaurant the Diamond Grill.

No one knows where the residential ghost of the Diamond Grill, "Stella," came from. There are reports of seeing Stella and visitors feeling things around them. This is especially noteworthy upstairs in the famous "Tudor Room." Stella is famous for taking "shiny objects," such as jewelry, and the objects are never to be found again. Some say that there have often been reports of a black mass in the Tudor Room and the candlesticks moving on their own.

*The Diamond Grill*

According to the reports from the LSP, (See the prior chapter for details of this organization) website, then (2010) special event manager, Ashley, reported to the team that she did not experience anything out of the ordinary personally, however, she has received many reports from the patrons and staff that there have been things moving around and disappearing. Patrons and the staff all report there was something going on in the Tudor Room as well as in the mezzanine/bar area.

One of the more interesting sightings that Ashley reported was of seeing a beautiful young Victorian woman dressed in Victorian-era clothes, with visitors being touched or having someone "watch" them.

According to the LSP website, the members of the Central Louisiana team include:

Grady Welch, Case Manager
Bree Hegwer, Co-Case Manager and Lead Investigator
Amber Wisinger, Investigator
Len Binning, Investigator

On Sept 19, 2020, the LSP investigators went to investigate the Diamond Grill restaurant. The investigators involved were Welch, Hegwer, and two individuals named "Michael" and "Lisa." Their fascinating report from their website is as follows:

> Equipment used: handheld recorder, K2 meter, camera, several deer cameras, handheld camera with night vision, and a digital still camera. We proceeded with our base line sweeps for EMF in all areas. While doing the walk through, we also took pictures. After the walk through, we proceeded to set up all equipment. On the second floor, in the Tudor Room, we started our investigation by setting up four deer cameras. Two in one room and two in the other room. We captured three EVPs in these rooms. First was a growl, second was an unexplained noise that we could not make out, and third was a jingling sound that sounded like keys but none of us were moving. We also captured an unknown light in the right-center

> of the frame on a deer camera that goes bright and fades. No idea (what it could be). The last thing we had was our K2 meter sitting by itself on a table and it started to just flash, again no idea on this one. Downstairs in the main dining room and bar area was the second part of our investigation. We once again set up our four deer cameras. One (was set up) in the bar. One (was set up) on the stairs leading to the bar. Another (was set up) in the hallway to the elevator. And the last (was set up) in the elevator itself. The elevator had been opening by itself on us all night, so we wanted to see if we could capture something. We did not get any EVPs on this part. But we got some pictures and videos. First, we have a picture of a shadow in the center mirror of the bar. There was no one up there at the time. Second, we have a video shot of the stairs; there is a loud banging noise and on the right side the light flashes quickly. Last, is a picture video of the elevator opening by itself. . . .

According to the *Town Talk*, "We had some good evidence there," said Grady Welch, case manager for the Central Louisiana Chapter of LSP. Welch's wife was the lead investigator of the organization.

While the group didn't encounter Stella during their visit, they did record three sounds. The report describes them as a growl, an unexplained noise, and what sounded like the jangling of keys. They also saw the elevator doors opening and closing on their own during the night they spent there, according to their report.

The LSP report concluded by saying, "In regard to the Diamond Grill, we strongly feel (paranormal) activity is prevalent here and we believe that with the help of a follow-up investigation, we will be able to get more evidence!"

The overall results of the investigation showed some paranormal activity at the Diamond Grill, but how the ghosts interacted with any visitors on any particular occasion was always different. You can't make them come out for you just because you want them to.

William A. "Bill" Tudor, son of Buddy Tudor, said in a *Town Talk* article that he was familiar with the story of Stella: "I don't know if I believe it, but it's great (publicity) for the city."

The interesting video of the ghost hunters shows the investigators taking data and exploring the Diamond Grill restaurant, from the kitchen to the Tudor Room. It is obvious from the video and the conversations between investigators that spirits do haunt the old pub. The video is well worth watching.

Scott Laliberte, president and chief operating officer for (Mike) Jenkins Companies which owns the Diamond Grill, said in a news release in 2024:

> The resident spirit that calls this place home has been nicknamed "Stella." She has been seen on several occasions as a well-dressed, sophisticated young woman. Stella is said to have a penchant for taking jewelry and placing it in other parts of the restaurant. In addition to her apparition being seen, staff have reported seeing a black mass on the third (floor). No one knows where the residential ghost, Stella, came from. Though there are reports of seeing Stella and feeling things around them, especially up in the famous Tudor Room, Stella is famous for taking shiny objects. Is Stella a long-lost patron still attached to this once-jewelry store? Who knows, but I highly recommend paying this place a visit. If you don't run into Stella, you can at least guarantee a wonderful dining experience!

The Diamond Grill is still open today and remains one of the most elegant and enjoyable restaurants in Louisiana. Go have a meal there and maybe you might meet some of the very longtime permanent guests of the Diamond Grill!

# Finnegan's Wake

## "Who Is Really There Having a Drink with You?"

According to the *Town Talk* newspaper in 2010, then Finnegan's Wake owners Shannon Nolan and Galen Bohannon "swear there's a ghost in their place that's scared the gin out of them." Nolan continued to say that the first time that he encountered whatever it was late one night when he played his violin in a bar. "He laid it down," he later said, "and then returned a minute later to find all four tuning pegs had been turned and a way-off-key sound coming from it."

Also according to the *Town Talk* newspaper, Nolan said "That just doesn't happen; It's never happened again. That was the first time I got the feeling that something was there. I left the building. It freaked me out."

Bohannon said one night that his back was to the racks of glasses at the bar when from behind him, unprovoked, a wine glass flew from the shelf, tumbled over his shoulder, and shattered on the ground. Nolan said, "The most common thing is the noises from the loft above the ceiling. We'll hear their tremendous noises upstairs. We go up and there's nothing disturbed."

The video of the *Ghost Hunters* show from 2011 (see the prior chapter on the Hotel Bentley for details) shows the investigators taking data and exploring Finnegan's Wake pub. It is obvious from watching the video and the conversations between investigators that some spirits do haunt the old pub. The video is well worth watching.

The *Ghost Hunters* show premiered on television on February 23, 2011, and was seen by nine million viewers. Viewing parties were held throughout Central LA, including a large party at the Diamond Grill restaurant.

According to the website "Haunted Nation":

> Prior to Finnegan's, the building was known as the Riverside Pub. Even prior to that, it was an optometrist office, which later moved to Jackson Street and became Vision Source. Staff have reported glasses sliding off shelves and a musician once claimed that his guitar was purposely detuned when no one was around to touch it.

One last story on Finnegan's Wake: Jan Wilson Farmer of Hineston, LA, said she was once at Finnegan's Wake when the following happened. She was sitting at a table when a strange shadow came across her table over her. She looked up and nothing was there. She strongly feels it was of the spirit world.

Finnegan's Wake pub, formerly located at 812 Third Street in Alexandria, has since closed for unknown reasons. Could it have closed, like the prior establishments there, for spiritual reasons?

# The Speakeasy

## "The Spirits Continue to Party"

One of the strangest places in all of Central Louisiana that I have personally visited and experienced was a place that I never expected to even exist—a 1920s speakeasy. What is a speakeasy you may ask? It is not a term commonly used anymore, particularly by the younger folk. But there are new bars and lounges that are now popping up around the nation that are priding themselves by calling themselves speakeasies.

I recently "discovered" that Alexandria, of all places, likely had a "speakeasy" of sorts. A speakeasy, also called a "blind pig," "blind tiger," or a "gin joint," is a place from the past where alcoholic beverages were illegally sold. In Alexandria's case, this establishment likely existed during Prohibition (1920-1933).

Speakeasies have a long history. A "speak softly shop," meaning a "smuggler's house," first appeared in a British slang dictionary in 1823. In the United States, the word first appeared in a newspaper article on March 21, 1889. The article referred to "speak easy" as the name for a saloon in the western Pennsylvania town that "sells without a license." Owner Kate Hester told her rowdy customers to "speak easy" to avoid unwanted attention from neighbors and the police.

But did Alexandria and Central Louisiana truly have its own speakeasy in the Roaring Twenties, a full century ago? Well, from all available accounts, it surely did, and more.

Not only did we likely have a speakeasy, but we may have had at least one brothel back then. This was fairly commonplace throughout the United States at that early time. Even New Orleans had the infamous neighborhood of "Storyville," one of the most famous "red-light" districts in the US where prostitution was effectively legal from 1897-1917.

I was recently given an exclusive, behind-the-scenes tour of what is hidden from the general public, a location deep underground within four blocks of the Alexandria city hall. The tour that I was given was truly one of the *most amazing tours of my life.* (I have been sworn to complete secrecy and cannot reveal the precise location, nor who has exclusive access and control to the location. This is for fear of people wanting/demanding to also have a tour of this potentially dangerous journey down deep underground.)

Quite frankly, I found this underground lair to be so spooky and eerie that it just boggles my mind that it really exists in this day and time. Only a horror movie set could even possibly replicate this setting.

First, let me describe the general area. Visiting this prominent old downtown Alexandria building, one would not expect a below ground lair. In Louisiana, buildings having basements are incredibly rare due to a high water level/table in the ground and frequent hard rains. I found the first floor of this building to be old-style construction, yet somewhat recently updated and quite functional. At first, there was nothing visible or noteworthy of the building that belies the fact that there are hidden rooms or hidden underground chambers. The tour guide who took me on this excursion walked me to this very unassuming door which I expected to open to be a closet or a small storage room. There were no markings or signs saying that one would soon be going deep underground. The tour guide pulled out an old, well-worn ring of keys from their pocket, selected a very particular, worn, large brass-colored key, and inserted it into the doorknob. Initially looking inside, all was dark, a midnight dark. The guide slipped their hand inside the door and flipped a switch. A single light bulb, hanging precariously from the ceiling, flipped on. I could tell it was an old-style bulb as the filament was bright and clearly distinguishable unlike bulbs of today.

Walking down a very tight, very steep, old, worn marble staircase, lit only by this old light bulb, the tour guide and I had to walk down very carefully, mostly holding on to the sides of the staircase's walls that had no railing. The worn marble steps below my feet were uneven and dipped in the center. It was clear to me that thousands of fancy leather shoe soles scrapped a path on the stairs going downward and upward on these stairs. And unrelentingly downward the steps went. It looked at first that we were going at least two stories down, but it was probably a bit less. It was all just so disorienting not to be able to initially see the bottom of the staircase, not to be able to gauge its depth. It felt so creepy going into the pitch-black darkness of this burrow,

*The stairs leading to the speakeasy*

seeing things that haven't seen the light of day since the time of President Calvin Coolidge and the notorious "flapper" girls of the era swinging their beaded headgear, gowns, and purses. The air was stale and dusty, but generally breathable. But it was the unknown ahead of me that most concerned me.

Arriving at the bottom was a slightly lit room off the staircase, lit by another hanging bulb of low wattage like the ones you would always see in a good horror or suspense movie. The light from the bulb was not enough to extend much into the next room, so what laid beyond there was unknown, at least for now. The room itself was more recently plastered over brick with much of the plaster now missing. This gave the walls the appearance that led to my impression of what one could feel visiting an excavation of Egyptian tombs, just without any Egyptian carved ornamentation. The shadows in the room were long as there were various odd boxes and building renovation supplies strewn throughout the room between the shadows, with no particular rhyme or reason to their placement. The light from the hanging bulb was so weak that it discouraged me and probably anyone else who was visiting from roaming around this room to explore. Who knows what was behind the boxes and supplies?! I learned that it was best just to stay where I had entered the room, not to explore it in depth. When I asked the guide where specifically the speakeasy area was, the guide pointed to what was obviously at one time a large passageway that was now securely plastered over in recent years. Was there a long walnut bar inside? With shelving racks for the one-time illegal hooch? Was there a mirror and/or a painting of a reclining nude woman behind the wall? The guide was unsure, but thought there might be so. This now-plastered opening headed in the direction going under the old, famed brick streets of Alexandria, a fact that was well publicized when I was a child in the early 60s. "Alexandria has more exposed brick streets that any other city in Louisiana" is what I was told many decades ago. And many less traversed streets are still paved with bricks that have shaken many a vehicle's shock-absorbers. But that is another story.

I continued to follow the guide when she said she was taking me to an area that was believed to have held a brothel. A brothel? Really? Wow! A brothel, a term rarely used today, also known as a cathouse, bordello, ranch house, or best yet, a whorehouse, is defined as a place where people engage in sexual activity with prostitutes. Although many a prominent citizen in Alexandria over the decades has been arrested for solicitation of a prostitute, I never expected to find an "official" place for prostitution here in Alexandria! As interesting as knowing about a speakeasy being here, I was actually even more surprised about having a brothel.

Upon entering this very long hallway that allegedly held the brothel, I could tell I was headed in another direction more toward the center of the old building that was above me. I could see at the end of this long hallway another hanging ceiling light in the far distance. It was like looking down a long dark tube with a tiny speck of light at the end. As I walked so very carefully down this very dark hallway, I was stepping carefully for fear of tripping over some unknown object, or even some little night creature that lived there. As my eyes got used to this even darker area, I could now tell there were alternating rooms on each side of the hallway. It was hard to tell how many rooms, but the rooms were just too dark to safely walk into. (The only light that I had was the little light that came from my cell phone.) What was in these rooms, I don't really know, but I just imagine the unusual and antiquated treasures that were still stored in each room. One room was actually lit by another one of those now famous hanging ceiling lights. And what I saw in it did amaze me. In this one room were what was once elegant marble, a handsome wooden door with opaque glass keeping one from seeing what was inside. There was a bathroom too dirty and cluttered to enter. I thought back and imagined the beautiful baths of past times and could also imagine the elegant boudoirs. The quietness and seclusion here was astonishing and breathtaking. I had to remind myself that I was deep underground while the world above continued its daily routine. This was a different world, a world the public did not want to know about, then and now, but was whispered about among a select few. What stories the brick walls and marble floors, the opaque windows and ancient wooden doors could now tell! The famous, and infamous, have trodden the carefully laden tile marble floors. The secret words given for entry, the coded knocks, the transaction of money, the music, all took place here in seclusion deep below the ground.

What was once probably the speakeasy section of this underground lair is now walled off, hidden for a future archaeologist to find and uncover one day. What kind of mahogany bar did it have, with the back wall lined with the very "freshest made" illegal booze then available? All here is locked away, back in the deep unrelenting dark for a future tomb raider-type explorer to one day again uncover.

The alleged brothel section was more accessible, but no more clear as it was mostly stripped away of its finest glory days. The tour guide said all evidence pointed to the use of this facility for the "enjoyment" of men, but that use was of a previous time. These rooms were no longer attractive to the eye or to the heart or the wants of man.

At the end of this dark hallway was once again a lit room, a room also crowded with storage. The room overall was less appealing, but the largest room I found. Visible though were some treasures of local history that I cannot share here as it may identify the controller of this underground lair. But I pawed through some of the items and was pleasantly surprised that they existed. But they were not disassembled parts of the one-time alleged speakeasy or brothel. Just off this room was another marble staircase, identical to the one that I came down on. Not one, but two marble staircases! Upon carefully rising to the top of this staircase, I re-entered the building above, but on a different side of the building. I would have been completely lost except for my guide. I thanked my guide for this truly amazing tour and thought for a moment about what I saw and then left.

Upon further thinking about this incredible trip, I realized one thing; something was completely off kilter. My guide and I always stayed close to each other while traversing this dungeon. Although I wasn't always looking at my guide, if I suddenly looked for them, I know I would find them within a second or two.

But here's the real spirited problem: while down there deep underground, I felt what I thought was the guide being in a certain area near me. But when I looked up to find the guide, the guide wasn't where I had felt them to be! They were elsewhere! It wasn't the guide's fault or actions that made me think they were in a certain place. It was something else, a heavy presence of some sort, best described as a third person. Yes, I felt someone else was there, not a malicious presence, but more of a watcher, a silent partner, a lonely companion. And the tour guide felt it too on their trips down deep. The temperature should have been all the same down there, but at times, I rubbed my hands and arms because it felt cold while other times down there it was humid and warmish. There was somebody or something down there walking along with us and watching what we were doing in their permanent home. Maybe a flapper, a bar patron, a prostitute, or something else, I don't know. But as interesting as it was visiting this long-forgotten den of iniquity, I don't want to ever go there again. I don't recommend that the reader try to find this place; just know that it is creepy, eerie, and apparently inhabited by the past people who wanted to enjoy life, and apparently still are!

# The Myrtle Groves Huie-Dellmon House

## "The Pages of the Book Continue to Turn by an Unknown Hand."

The Myrtle Groves Huie-Dellmon House, better known as the Huie-Dellmon House, located at 421 Lee Street is a historic survivor in downtown Alexandria. With so many old homes discarded over the years by thoughtless hands, the Huie and Dellmon families decided to save this petit, yet remarkable home and donate it for public use, now used as the Rapides Parish Library headquarters.

Built in 1897 in the Gilded Age by Henarie M. Huie (1861-1926), the co-founder of the *Town Talk* newspaper in 1883, the house was first lived in by Huie and his wife, Margaret Jane "Maggie" Brown Huie (1862-1932), and their family. When Huie's daughter, Myrtle Groves Huie (1897-1970), married Joseph "Joe" Dellmon (1896-1976) in 1918, they lived in the house along with her parents. All became involved in the management of the newspaper. Myrtle herself would eventually succeed her mother and sister, Vera Huie Wilson (1889-1937), and become the president of the *Town Talk* publishing company, McCormick and Company Inc., serving as president from 1937-1966. Myrtle and Joe Dellmon, who had no children, lived in the home until their respective deaths. They established a trust for their estate, and the trust donated the house to the parish library system in 1993. In March of 2017, the house was granted National Register of Historic Places status by the US Park Service based upon Myrtle Dellmon's significant contributions to her community in the field of communications.

The outside of the house was extensively altered by the Dellmons with a brick veneer, but the inside remains, for the most part, as it originally looked.

*The Huie-Dellmon House*

When the house was donated, the furniture and possessions in the Huie-Dellmon House were also donated, giving the house an air of early-twentieth-century life. Stepping into the house, one truly feels that they are stepping back in time. Myrtle's hand in decorating the house is quite evident with her delicate vases and other decorative ceramics displayed on and inside of gingerbread-style furniture. The inside design scheme is noted as quite unusual, though with many, maybe too many, doors and closets shared by opposite rooms that one can walk through to go room by room. Though the house is not particularly large, one can still almost get lost in it.

The strong and vibrant long lives of the Huies and the Dellmons truly left an eternal mark on the house, a mark evident by many spiritual happenings in the house. Celise Reech Harper, the director of the Rapides Parish Library system since January 2020, has a lot to say about the spirit world of the house, as have many others.

> Since my appointment, I've heard numerous stories regarding a possible presence of Miss Myrtle (Dellmon), who was the former resident of this facility. It was her home. I believe she was the first female editor of the Alexandria *Town Talk*. Her family owned this property as well as adjoining properties.
>
> As far as spooky happenings go, I've been told many stories about doors opening whenever someone was here alone. I can tell you a humorous incident where I was here late one evening with one other employee where we were having a conversation and we both jumped out of our skin whenever one of the doors farther down the hall managed to swing open. This is an old drafty building, and there is always the propensity that when one door opens just enough when you haven't properly closed another, it might cause the other door to swing open. There are always explanations that can exist, but it is fun to think about that the essence or presence of those who came before us and did good work here are still here and exist in the building.
>
> We've had several longtime employees who claim that they have had instances where they have turned off the water in the bathroom

> only to later have the water turn back on again (without them being there). We've had multiple people discuss the doors, really big doors, opening and closing with no one there. We have also had people claiming instances where they have heard things, heard footsteps or felt a strong presence in the building. A lot of longtime employees have said they have experienced things of that nature. I personally have not experienced things of that higher level. . . .

Wes Saunders, longtime assistant parish library director, has much to say about the spirit world at the Huie-Dellmon House:

> It has always been my understanding that the name of the ghost was Myrtle. Apparently Myrtle was the lady of the house at one time. My experience with her ghost or ghost-like apparitions or what have you is that I have been in the Huie-Dellmon House and was the only person in the building at the time and heard footsteps. The hearing of footsteps in the house while I am standing still, it's not me, it's not an echo, there was someone else in there, but I was the only (living) person in the building.
>
> I have heard from previous employees that they have noticed things in the house that were moved in their offices. This occurred over the weekends when nobody was in there; no employees overnight or such. They would see (for example) a vase would be moved from one place to another in their office or some such item moved like a lamp. Also, small pieces of furniture would be moved. There was no good explanation as to how or why for the movement. There are some people who no longer work here at the library that may have some more details as to their interaction with the ghost because everybody who has worked there (at the Huie-Dellmon House) without exception has had some kind of strange happenings occur to them. Steve Rogge and Laura Ellen Ayres (both former library directors there) will have some stories to (potentially) tell. . . .

Jan Wilson Farmer of Alexandria and now Hineston, who held many positions with the Rapides Parish Library system during her forty-three years with the library, the last being the Book Mobile manager, spoke about her experiences and other past employee experiences at the Huie-Dellmon House:

I worked in the Huie-Dellmon House for about two and a half years serving as the liaison to the Friends (of the Rapids Parish Library) group and several others. Whenever I was alone in the house, a buzzer would go off, like a servant's bell buzzer. I knew it had been taken out as I saw it had been taken out because we kept up with what was going on in the house when they were renovating it for our offices. So (on this day), I was by myself and was locked in. The buzzer goes off and I go to the front door and see that nobody was there. So, I sit back down at my desk and the buzzer goes off a. ain. No one was there again. And finally, after a couple of days of this, I stood up (from my desk) and addressed who I thought it was by name and said, 'Please stop ringing the buzzer; I'm not your servant. Get whatever you need.' And the buzzer ringing stopped.

I always felt welcome in the house. It always welcomed me. . . . I knew the history of the house. I knew the history of the land (the house sits on) and of the work sheds sitting on. There had been an (automotive repair) garage there at one time by Mr. (Joseph) Dellmon and my grandfather took his car there to be repaired. That was where the parking lot is across from the library. It was not concrete then, it was gravel and dirt. There was a big oak tree that sat in the corner of the street where my grandfather would put me down in the roots of the oak tree and played with rocks there until my grandfather and Mr. Dellmon were finished working on the car.

I always felt that I had a close connection with this house. I never felt scared when I was alone, just sometimes a bit annoyed because of the (ringing of the) bell once in a while but never threatened. I love the house, and it was kind of sorrowful for me to take another position (outside of the house), but I knew that I was always welcomed to come back by the house. I have always had the feeling of comfort that whatever was (inhabiting there) would always let me come back.

Now I have been present when people would come into the house to visit (attending meetings and such) . . . and they would step back and say that they cannot enter the house because they felt a brick wall. So we accepted that. We had a couple of people come in and they would turn around and say that they had to leave. Literally, the hair on the back of their necks and on their arms would be standing straight up. They would then leave with no explanation. I realize that is common when you don't understand.

> Somebody told me, and I don't know how true this is, that since your body is made up of electricity that sometimes people who die don't realize that they are dead, and they stay around in the place that they are comfortable with. And if there is an intruder sometimes, they can feel the anger. But I never felt there was anger here. You keep your mind open to everything. Yes, I'm a Christian. Do I believe in ghosts? Yes! Because I feel that some people have not crossed over for whatever reason yet.

Jan also told the story of polishing the antique furniture in the meeting room of the house. She would do this every day at one point. But no matter where she would place the decor plates and platters, the plates and platters would mysteriously be moved the next morning. This was actually a common occurrence in the house. So one day, Jan spoke directly to the ghosts and said something like that she "thanked the ghosts for redecorating the house." She also said to "put the dishes and platters where they wanted them to go" and that she (Jan) "would leave them alone." The dishes and platters stopped moving around after that.

Jan also shared other staff accounts. She said that the late Sharon McMonagle who used to have an office in the Huie-Dellmon House was in the office alone one day. She saw out of the corner of her eye a tall person, a man, looking out of the side window at the front door of the house. By the time Sharon turned her head to get a better look, the ghostly man had disappeared.

Jan always felt that the spirit world in the house was not threatening and was almost friendly.

Beth Vandersteen of Poland, LA, was also a former administrative staff member at the Rapides Parish Library whose office was at one time in the Huie-Dellmon House. She later became the director of the West Baton Rouge Parish Library in Port Allen, LA, and is now retired. She says of the spiritual happenings at the Huie-Dellmon home:

> I was alone in the Huie-Dellmon House on a Friday afternoon. For some reason other staff members had something to do and the house was empty except for me. I was working on some project that I was determined to finish before I got off from work at four o'clock that day. I was sitting at my computer in what was the former dining room of the Huie-Dellmon House where my office was located. I was just hammering away at the computer trying to get my project

tied together and finished. I heard footsteps come from the back door through the kitchen, up the hall, past my door, and into what was the front sunroom (now the library's meeting room) of the house. It sounded like a lady walking in high heel shoes and a man walking in leather sole shoes right behind her. They were walking with purpose; they weren't hurrying per se. And I thought: Okay, the (back) door has a buzzer on it when it opens, and I didn't hear the buzzer go off. I said (to myself) let me see who's in here now. And there was no one in there or anywhere in the house. I was the only one in the house. The sounds had been so clear that I really put the brakes on the project and promptly left. It freaked me out as it was so clearly a woman in high heels and a man in leather sole shoes going from the back to the front of the house. And it gave me the creeps. . . .

I felt like it was Myrtle (Huie) Dellmon and Mr. (Joe) Dellmon walking. When we received the house (as a donation from the family), we received everything still in it, the vases, the glassware, and such. Everything (of theirs) was still there including their scrapbooks and photos. (We could see from their scrapbooks) That they loved to entertain, they loved to have people (visit). . . .

(The late) Sharon (McMonagle) told me that she saw the telephone move one time in the front sunroom as well as a lot of things that just moved around by themselves that we didn't know why. . . .

I used to do book discussion groups supported by grants with the Louisiana Endowment for the Humanities (LEH) and they generally lasted six weeks. People would register for the class, pick up three or four books that they would read, and discuss as a group over a six week period. We would generally meet on a Tuesday or Thursday night. At one of the meetings, we had a security guard because of where the Huie-Dellmon House is located. I decided that I wouldn't be there by myself, as I had had a bad experience at the main library at one time. So I wanted to hire a deputy to be on the house and grounds while everyone was here and to make sure everyone gets in their cars (safely) after it was over. His first name was Jasper. He was a super, super guy. He provided security that night. He would sit in the kitchen and every once in a while would make a round in the parking lot and make sure no one was messing with the cars or anything. So, when we finished the program and everybody went home, I was putting the food away and Jasper was just sitting in a chair at the kitchen table. (I looked at him and saw that) He was

> white as a sheet. I finished putting the food away and he was still sitting there saying nothing, so I said, "Are you okay?" He said, "It is a strange night." I asked him what happened. It should be noted that it had been raining all day and was gray and droopy outside with mist and fog. He said, "Well, while I was out making the usual rounds walking around the property, I saw this light coming up the street in front of the Huie-Dellmon House coming from the (Red) river end of the street. I thought it was odd, as it was only one light, and I didn't hear a motorcycle engine. There was no noise, and this light was like a ball (orb) of light coming up the road. I stood there and watched it. When it got to the edge of the fence (in front of the house), all of a sudden, the ball of light shot straight up to the top of the tree over there.
>
> "You know there are some really big trees on the property." Jasper continued,
>
> "The light finally faded. It was the strangest thing. There was no sound. It couldn't have been reflections. There was no cars driving up the street. I don't know what that was. And it just freaked me out. . . ."
>
> So you have an officer of the law that can't explain what happened on a misty night at the Huie- Dellmon House. It must have been a fifolet.

So Myrtle and Joe still maintain their home and guard their possessions in the Huie-Dellmon home, forever and ever. . . .

**WRITER'S NOTE:** According to Cajun folklore, the fifolet is said to be the ghostly spirit of a person who died a violent death, either by drowning in the swamps or through some other tragic event.

# Kent House

## "The Baillio Family Still Awaits You to Come and Visit"

Like Loyd Hall, Kent House at 3601 Bayou Rapides Road in Alexandria is an amazing Louisiana treasure trove of history. Every day, the tour guides there show visitors how life was like two hundred years ago, both the good life as well as the bad life. Although an irreplaceable historic treasure, Kent House should also be remembered as the family home of many families over the decades, especially the Baillios and the Hynsons.

Kent House is a historic masterpiece that is located just off the busy MacArthur Drive in Alexandria. Even if it were not unique in having survived both the devastation of the passage of time and of the Civil War, Kent House would be remarkable for its magnificent architecture alone. The house is regarded as the oldest standing structure in North Louisiana. It is also an excellent example of eighteenth-century rural Louisiana plantation architecture. Built between 1796 and 1800 by Pierre Baillio Sr., the house was a more simple structure than we see today. Subsequent owners in 1842 added additional rooms and refinements for style and accommodation.

Both in plan and construction, Kent House is a fine example of French and Spanish colonial construction. The house is constructed as a raised cottage with the living quarters well above the ground on brick piers. Heavy cypress timbers form the framework which is held together with wooden pegs, many of which can still be seen on the exterior. The walls of the house were completed by filling the spaces between the timbers with a mixture

*Kent House*

of mud, moss, and deer hair, then called "*bousillage*" by the French. The exterior walls are finished only with a thin coating of plaster or layers of lime-wash to better protect the exposed areas from the weather.

Materials used for creating this elegant home come from the surrounding area including the previously mentioned mud, plant, and animal materials. The native clay was baked in the sun to provide the unique rose-colored bricks we see today. Timbers from nearby trees were used to frame the house.

The house was originally built a short walking distance away from the current site, just across the busy MacArthur Drive, that original location also facing Bayou Rapides as the house still faces today. In 1961, the house was then in use as a VFW (Veterans of Foreign Wars) meeting building. But by then, the veterans had long outgrown the then antiquated 170-year-old building, and there was even talk of its demolition. But the good ladies of the local Colonial Dames organization lead the way in obtaining money and resources to move and to restore this one-of-a-kind building. It must have been amazing to see back then this house being moved in parts across MacArthur Drive to its new and now permanent home. Over the years, various generous donations of old plantation buildings, including two enslaved peoples' homes, a kitchen, a milk house, and other such buildings have formed a circular "village" of sorts of buildings to the rear of the house.

Driving through Alexandria, one simply turns off MacArthur Drive onto historic Bayou Rapides Road, not far from where LA Highway 28 going west is located. On Bayou Rapides, one sees a long road of beautiful and historic houses as well as plantation homes. Bayou Rapides was a main river thoroughfare of sorts in nineteenth-century Central Louisiana. Dozens of historic plantation homes were located along this busy waterway, now called a bayou, many of which were burned by Union troops during the Civil War. But Kent House was saved, likely by the then owner, a man named Robert Hynson, signing an amnesty oath at the end of the war pledging his allegiance to the United States. Hynson signed the oath in order to save his home, but he would never know that his saving his home would serve to protect this diamond among the many well-known Louisiana plantation homes of yore.

After passing a house or two onto Bayou Rapides Road, one is suddenly confronted with the shaded darkness of ancient oak trees overhanging the street. Approaching the front of the plantation home, one clearly feels like they are entering a time machine and returning back to colonial times. Entering the driveway and passing by an old-style picket fence, one is again confronted with this unimaginable grand site of an eye-catching house. Grand may not be the word for what one sees when they see this house built before Louisiana was even a part of the United States. Quite frankly, this writer cannot describe the true awe of seeing it. Added to the impressive structural allure is that this home is now nearly 230 years old! What this house must have seen in its twenty-three decades! What bodies figuratively lie deep below its still sturdy bricks! No wonder the ghost and spirit stories flourish here! If one is expecting to encounter the spirit world, this is truly the place to go!

LeAnn Raines is the senior tour director there now. She is a delightful person to meet and visit with. She knows the secrets of Kent House like no one else alive knows because she has experienced them herself and has heard from hundreds of others who have experienced ghostly dealings. A native of Alexandria, she loves Louisiana history and is often contacted by people needing answers to historical matters in Central Louisiana. When asked what brought her to Kent House, she saw an ad once asking for volunteers to come work there. This volunteership evolved into a longtime job where she has met thousands of visitors representing nearly every country in the world. She says, "What I like most about giving tours here is meeting people from all over the world. They learn the history of Kent House and Central Louisiana from me, and I learn of their home and country from them."

What LeAnn doesn't like as much is the spirit world that continues to inhabit Kent House. She has a lot to say about the residents "living" at Kent House:

> I was here working for six months when I had my first experience. I had no prior experience with the paranormal and wasn't expecting to ever have an experience. It was 4:00 p.m. one day and I was working with Sandy Lott (a former tour guide there) when I went to lock up the gift shop. (The gift shop then was one of the 1830 era slave cabins that came from Augusta Plantation.) Well, I was walking toward the house when I saw an image under the outdoor porch area. The image appeared just five feet away from me. The image was of a human torso. It was not transparent, but real as

plain as day. It looked like a Union officer's coat. It was navy blue with two rows of buttons. There were no legs or arms or head that I saw. When I later had watched the movie Glory I saw actor Matthew Broderick wearing the same coat, so I knew it was a Union officer's coat. I stopped the video to examine the coat, and it was the exact same. When I saw it floating at Kent House, I instantly froze. I literally stopped in my tracks. This image was so realistic and stayed floating for about three seconds and then it disappeared. I stood there for a long while as it had shocked me so much. I asked myself did I really see it. When I regained my composure, I continued my duty to lock up the outbuildings around Kent House. It was at least a year and a half before I told anyone of this story as I didn't want anyone to think I was strange.

When I had been working at Kent House for only four weeks, I gave a tour to two gentlemen from Chicago. One was white and one was black. I took them on the standard tour, and everything was normal at first. We went through the main part of the house and ended up in the library (also known as Robert Hynson's 1795-1875 office) which was the route of the standard tour. When we went into the room, I noticed immediately the black gentleman had an odd look about him. He stepped back suddenly from the other fellow. I continued giving my talk on the room and I noticed that the black gentleman started looking ashen in color of his skin. I thought he was going to pass out. He then quickly bent down and grabbed fully with his right hand his neck. When I saw that, I immediately stopped giving my talk and asked him to sit on a nearby bench on the front porch just out of the library door. I told him to relax there, and I then ran down to the kitchen to get him a bottle of water. I returned and gave him the bottle, thinking he was overheated. He said, "No ma'am, I am not overheated. I suddenly felt a crushing feeling in my chest." The black gentleman said he was a critical care nurse, and he knew what he was feeling. The gentleman then became emotional and pointed to the library door and said that there was something in the library that did not want him in there. He then said, "You probably think I'm crazy and don't believe me." I said, "I do believe you—please tell me what you experienced in there." He then told me that when he entered the room, he felt this crushing feeling on his chest and just could not breathe. I told him that we do not have to continue this tour and we could go back to the shop and I would refund his money to him. He said that was not necessary, but adamantly said, "Someone is in that room and doesn't want me in there and I refuse to go back in that room." We then continued on the tour without further incident.

Other people have told me on tours that they have felt an angry presence and didn't want to enter. This fear of entering that room because of an evil spirit was most common in that room. At least one person, likely more than one person, has died in the house.

There are so many spirit events here that I hope to be able to tell them all. On tours, I have had people literally from all over the world, who have never met one another, tell me that there is a gentleman that follows me through the house (while on tours). And he follows me from the Artifact Room, but he stops at the girl's room door. The visitors will describe what he is wearing; they all give the same description. This person who follows me wears a colonial-type garb. They tell me he is an older man. They say he will follow me when I stop on a tour that I am giving, that he will smile and will look at me. Then he will look out one of the house's windows. And when people tell me that, I ask the visitors if they know what he is looking for. I ask them if they know what else he is looking at. And they will tell me that this gentleman, this spirit doesn't recognize the buildings outside as the set up looks now. (The back buildings, including the kitchen, slave cabins, the barn and blacksmith shop were moved to the Kent House grounds from other area plantation homes.) He seems to be wondering where the buildings he had built are now, because he does not recognize the buildings present. This is long before I had even got to the outside part of the tour where I tell the tour guests that none of the current historic buildings in the back of the house are original to Kent House. So the visitors on tour have no way of knowing that these other buildings are original with Kent House. This spirit is very likely that of the first owner and is the builder of Kent House, Pierre Baillio Sr.

I've also had people on two different occasions tell me that there is a gentleman walking behind me on the outside portion of the tour. He starts from under the house where I start the outside portion of the tour and follows me through all of the outside tour. But usually when I get to the old gift shop (one of the two 1830s slave cabins), the spirit gentleman will then walk back to the house. When we were working inside the old gift shop (the enslaved peoples' cabin), at least two times a week we would see a figure go in front of the window, Alice (Scarborough, Kent House executive director) has seen it also, and always go in the direction of the main house. This was so common that the tour guides, including myself, would look at each other and ask, "What was he (the spirit) wearing today?" One of us would describe the color of the shirt and it was always what the other tour guide saw. Always. The color of the spirit's shirt was normally bluish in color; that is what I saw most of the time. But whatever he was wearing, he was always going in the direction toward the main house. Many different visitors have also told me about seeing this gentleman who follows me outside; that he walks around checking his property. That figure, if he is different, apparently recognizes some of the buildings here or for some reason he just likes to walk the grounds. I don't know for sure. The visitors tell me he doesn't go in the house so he might be a different figure than the figure who follows me in the house.

When we were decorating for the candlelight tour last year, of course in the house we decorate with fresh fruit as that would be what the early residents of the house would use to decorate. So I was in the parlor of the house all alone at about ten o'clock in the morning. I was placing oranges and satsumas on the garland that was on the mantel in the parlor. I stood back to make sure that everything was even and on the right side of the mantel, one of the oranges flew off the mantel. It did not fall downward; it flew across the room and hit the door that enters into the back gallery. Literally, it flew horizontally across the room and hit the door. I stood there amazed; I didn't know what to do. I assume one of the permanent residential spirits was displeased about something, so I wasn't sure if I should go and pick up the orange and place it back or just leave the house. So I stood there for about a minute and slowly went over and picked up the orange and then placed it in a different position. It stayed in that position.

I don't ever have an uneasy feeling being in the home. One of my coworkers who doesn't work here anymore on occasion did not feel at ease going into the house and did not want to go in the house by herself. She didn't understand why I didn't feel anything bad there. When I asked her to describe what she felt and she said it was a "heaviness." Often we would go unlock the house together and she would say something like, "Oh, there're at home today."

But I make it a habit ever since I started working here, when I go into the house the first time in the morning, I would tell the spiritual community, "Good Morning." We always do. I would tell them good morning. As far as I'm concerned that is their home and I represent it respectfully and accurately the way it should be.

Last fall of 2022, October or November, for some reason very often for a month or so we would hear a very loud noise in the house that sounded like a large table was being drug across the wood floor. I have even heard it downstairs while I had a tour group with me. The tourists have heard it also and they would ask me, "What was that noise in the house?" My own sister heard it when she came here helping us hang the garlands on the gallery at Christmastime. We have gone up to the house in the mornings where on two or three occasions, the bolts were all slid inside the house and we couldn't get in. The other doors were padlocked and the padlocks were untouched. There is only one way to slide the bolts and that is to be inside the house. So, using the clack in the door, we would first undo the outside padlock and then literally get a butter knife and spend upward to an hour trying to pry that bolt open and slide the bolt back into place in order to get in.

I've seen things move in the home, including artifacts placed in different places. I've found candlesticks on one particular table in the parlor by the window moved. I've opened up the library (Robert Hynson's office) on a few occasions and found the candlesticks there on the secretary where you walk in, to the right of the room. I've found them on the opposite side of the room on the floor. I would pick them up, place them back. On one occasion on the very next morning, the same candles were out of the candleholders, and they were placed on the desk beside the brass candleholder that they were in.

The Artifact Room (originally the main bedroom in the original portion of the house) visitors tell me that they feel a presence in that room. I have never mentioned anything of a paranormal nature on a tour, ever. People ask me frequently if the house is haunted. The most I tell them that it's not haunted; to me that's such a negative connotation. Is there a presence here, very much so. I have obviously experienced that, but in the Artifact Room, people feel a heaviness, right at the entrance to the boy's room. They (the visitors) tell me when they stand there that they feel something very strong in that room. I've heard that very often about that room. That room and the girl's room. Very frequently people tell me that they feel a heaviness in that room. They feel that someone had experienced a prolong illness that ended in death in that room.

And the one experience that sticks out in my mind happened maybe about six months ago (in 2023). I had an entourage here from Fort Polk (now Fort Johnson in nearby Leesville, Louisiana). One man was a battalion commander from Fort Polk, and he had the commander of the Columbian military that was a guest here, along with his wife. So, we had an interpreter also. We are used to getting these type of people here. I led them into the girl's room on my regular tour. They all spoke Spanish. When they entered the room, they (the Columbians) all started speaking at once. I couldn't understand what they were saying so I asked the interpreter, "Is everything okay? Do they have questions?" He looked at them and he looked at me and said they (the Columbians) want you to know that there is a presence in this room. I said, "Can you describe it to me?" And he said yes, there is a very heavy presence in this room. At least one person or more than one person died in this room. Now mind you, all of these men were in uniform. They are all field grade officers. These are very accomplished men. But they told me that someone experienced a horrific death in this room. I hear that a lot. There's no real spiritual happenings in the out buildings.

There was a lady who came on the tour in the summer. During the tour when we came out of the library (Robert Hynson's office), She said, "Oh, that's so nice. I love how ya'll dress here." I said thank you. She said, "Well I like your dress too, but I'm talking about the lady standing by the door over there." And I looked over there and said, "There's a lady by the door?" She looked very surprised, like you don't see her? I said that I didn't see anyone. She said again, "She standing there now right by the door at the corner." I asked her to describe the woman standing to me. She that that the woman had a black dress on, that the dress was not really full, (and with) long sleeves. She said that the dress had black lace around the cuff with kind of a high collar with lace around the top. She said the woman was an older lady. I asked, "What is she doing?" She said she is just looking at us smiling. I said, "Okay. That is the next room that we have to go into. We are going to walk over there." We are in the master bedroom now. As we were going to walk in that direction,

I asked her to tell me what she does when we pass her, that I would appreciate knowing. So we got about half way and I asked what she was doing and the visitor said the woman was just fading away, but she is still smiling. I asked the visitor, "Do you know her name? Did you pick up on anything else about her?" She said to let her think and then she said, "I'm feeling like an S, like Sarah, or Sally, something of that type." Now I had never mentioned to this visitor about Sallie Hynson Ringgold (1848-1939) whose portrait is in the Artifact Room. So I brought the visiting woman into the Artifact Room and I showed her the portrait of Mrs. Ringgold that we have on display there and I asked the visitor, "Is this who you saw?" and she said, "Oh my gosh, the portrait is very similar to the woman that I saw." I told her that was Sallie Hynson Ringgold. We were both very surprised if not shocked at what had happened. When we got to the library, the lady said to me that there was a presence there. I feel like the presence doesn't want me here. She said that she felt a heaviness in her legs. She added that he (the spirit) was not in this room. I said, "Okay, but where is he?" I'm so thankful that a lot of times that there is no one else on the tour but these people who are experiencing this strange feeling. She said that he is downstairs under the house. She said that it's like this negative presence is radiating. I feel it, but he's not here on this floor. She asked me if there was another room below this and I answered no. (The house is raised off the ground and under the house is a walkable breezeway.) I told her that directly below where we are is near the steps going up the second (main) floor of the house.

People have told me all sorts of stories of their own personal spiritual experiences here. Last year I had five ladies from Iowa that came here. They also mentioned about the spiritual gentleman that follows me through the house while I am giving tours. But I didn't know that was going on in the house. I noticed one of the five ladies that didn't look particularly easy. I recognize that look now because I've done so many of these tours. At first I thought that she (the visitor) was bored maybe, but when we got downstairs, the rest of her friends said, "Well, Terry, what did you see in this house?" And she looked very aggravated when they said that. And they said, "Oh, come on, you had to have seen something. We could tell that you were feeling something." She said, "Ya'll stop. I don't want to talk about it." I told her, "No ma'am, it's okay if you want to talk about this. We hear things like this a lot." I said to her that I would really like it if she would share with me what she saw and knows if you did experience something on the tour in the house. She described that there are two people living there. I said okay. She further described that one is an elderly gentleman. She said that he follows me, and she described the same rooms, from the Artifact Room, but he does not go into the girl's room (which is near the end of the tour). She said he disappeared there. The other spiritual resident is a lady. She said that she doesn't know who she is, but that she is kind of middle aged. I said that is okay. I asked then to tell me about the gentleman. She said that he just follows me, walking about ten feet behind. When you stop, he stops. But she said that he likes you very much. He approves of you being here. I said (laughing a little) "That's always nice to hear!" She said that he very much appreciates that you are respectful of his home. I said, "Okay, do you know a name, can you tell me who he is?" She responded that she didn't know other than to say that he is an older gentleman, kind of like "old timey, 1776 era type clothes." So I assume it is Mr. (Pierre) Baillio (Sr.) following me around. She further said that he loves his home. They were very happy here. She said that was all she could really feel. She did add that there is another spiritual gentleman present on the property, but that he stays outside. She said that she is unclear as to who he is. The lady visitor's friend said that's all she talks about as she has a connection to the world of the dead. If there is something spiritual about an old house or place, she can connect and tell us all about her connection.

Another tour guide here said that several years ago on a tour had a girl, thirteen to fourteen years of age, start crying on the tour because something had "touched her" in the house. The tour guide didn't see anything and nothing was there to touch the young girl. On another tour several months ago, maybe as much as a year ago (in 2023), we had just finished the outside tour, specifically the sugar mill portion. We were then headed back to the old gift shop and a young lady in the tour group said, "That's really neat. I love how you have living history people here." I said well, we wear these dresses here every day to portray that era when people first were living in the house. She said, "No, I mean the man on the back porch there (on the second floor). I mean the man who is now watching us from the back porch." Of course, I looked up at the back porch and no one was there. I asked her if there was still a man on the porch. She looked at me confused, I guess wondering why I didn't clearly see him, (like) why are you asking me about the man who is clearly visible from where we stood. She said that he was at the door of the steps. She again asked me if I saw him and I responded no ma'am, I don't see him. I then asked her to describe him to me. She gave me a similar description to what (other) visitors had given me. She said he had a hat on, with a kind of a vest under a jacket. I asked her if his dress was like a colonial type of garb. She said no, not really, not like "13 colonies type." His dress was a bit later. I asked her, "What is he doing?" She said that he was just standing there with his hands on the railing and he was just watching us. I said okay. We continued standing there and she suddenly said, "Oh, now he's gone." I said, "Well, I hated that I didn't see that, but for some reason I just don't see that gentleman like others do."

I had a good friend that came here a couple of years ago and she brought her granddaughters with her on a tour. We came into the Artifact Room and everything was fine. When I moved on to the boy's room, the next room, I saw that she had a very odd look on her face. I go to church with her. And I could have dismissed her look at first, but she continued to look very bothered. You learn to recognize here when someone has a spiritual experience on the tour. You notice when their demeanor changes instantly. So I stopped and asked her if she was okay. She said, "You're going to think I'm crazy, but has anyone ever mentioned to you about something happening in this smaller room (the boy's room) and it being haunted?" And I responded, well sometimes. I then asked her, "What are you feeling?" She responded that there was a "heaviness" in that room. She said that there was someone in the room, that she could not see them, but that it was a very heavy, heavy presence. I asked, "Is it one person, two people?" She said that she thought it was one. She then said she had felt this before in other places all through my life, but wow, nowhere so strong as here. The presence here is very, very heavy in that room. She said, "Please don't think I'm crazy." And I said that I didn't and that I knew her well enough that she wasn't crazy. I told her that we hear this a lot at Kent House, and I definitely believe in what she was saying.

It's hard to determine which is the most haunted plantation home in Louisiana. I feel it's a tossup between Loyd Hall and Kent House, one getting first place and the other getting second place. These two historic residences are places that come as close to being "guaranteed" places you will most likely encounter spirits.

For an even stronger experience, try a candlelight tour at either. Have your car keys in your hand as when you leave, it will be very quickly!

# JAMES W. BOLTON HOUSE

## "WE ARE WATCHED OVER FOREVER"

James Calderwood Bolton (1899-1974), the builder of what is often referred to as the Bolton House, located at 900 City Park Blvd. in Alexandria, was a member of the third generation of the Bolton family living in Central Louisiana. His father, James Wade Bolton (1869-1936), is probably best known for his extensive service on the Rapides Parish School Board for the Central Louisiana community. He was elected to the board in 1904 and served until 1934, two years before his untimely death. During the time, Bolton served as president of the Rapides Parish School Board from 1916-1934, a total of eighteen years, longer than anyone else has ever chaired the board. Bolton High School on Vance Avenue was named after him as tribute to his many years of service while on the school board. It should be noted that the home of James Wade Bolton and his second wife, Mary Esther Calderwood Bolton (1876-1952), is now the home of River Oaks Square Art Center in downtown Alexandria.

James Wade's father and James C's grandfather was Colonel George Washington Bolton (1841-1931), a native of Georgia who fought for the Confederacy during the Civil War, but he is best known as the founder and director of the Rapides Bank & Trust Company of Alexandria. Most of the older Bolton family members are all buried in historic Mount Olivet Cemetery in Pineville.

James Calderwood Bolton (1899-1974), the builder and first owner of the Bolton House, was a banker by trade like his grandfather. He was associated with Rapides Bank & Trust Company from 1922-1974 (as an assistant cashier from 1922-1925, vice president from 1925-1936, president from 1936-1955, and as chairman and board of directors from 1956-1974). He was also the director of Delta Cotton Oil & Fertilizer Co. in Jackson, Mississippi; Louisiana Board of Public Welfare chairman from 1952-1956 and 1960-1964; Alexandria Civil Service Commission chairman from 1944-1970; and the Louisiana State University Foundation president from 1964-1965. He was instrumental in the founding of Louisiana State University of Alexandria and the LSU-A library is named in honor of him. He was active in the Alexandria Chamber of Commerce (president, 1930-1931); Louisiana Bankers Association (president, 1933-1934); and American Bankers Association (president of the state banking division, 1935). He also served his country during World War I in the US Army.

James Calderwood Bolton married Frances Elizabeth "Fran" Sample (1902-1986) on April 10, 1924. They were the parents of two children: Mary Eleanor Bolton (1927-1936) and Frances McCrory "Fran" Bolton Davis (1928-2016), who married Dr. Paul McMillian Davis Jr. (1919-2007). Fran Bolton Davis sold the Bolton home to the Pillarisetti family. This branch of the family is buried at Greenwood Memorial Cemetery in Pineville.

The land that the Bolton home is on was previously owned by was Constant Petrus Sr. (1876-1958), a native of Belgium. He had purchased a large tract of land on what was one time the outskirts of Alexandria. In February of 1939, a small parcel of land described as "the lower front corner of the Petrus estate fronting on Bayou Robert" was sold by Constant Petrus to Frances Sample Bolton for $2,560. By early 1940, the construction of the Bolton House was completed on this site. According to James Calderwood's first cousin, Roscoe Bolton (1913-2012), this house was built as a mirror image of some famous house in Hollywood, California.

During the Louisiana Maneuvers of the early 1940s, the Bolton home hosted many of the military elite as guests, many having afternoon tea with Mrs. Bolton. Fran M. Bolton Davis, daughter of the builder, remembered the connection her family home had to the Maneuvers in an interview before her death: "There were soldiers all over the place, camping on the bayou bank right next to our home on the edge of town," Fran said, "They had a mock battle between the Red and

*The Bolton House*

Blue armies battling over possession of our home," She said that the men had no place to shower, so the Boltons and their neighbors let the soldiers into their homes to shower.

James Calderwood Bolton was chairman of the war bonds committee during the war.

In 1974, after James C. Bolton died, his widow Fran continued to live there until she too passed away in 1986. During her later years living in the Bolton home, she had certain modifications done to the home making it more wheelchair accessible. After her death, her daughter hired what has been described as a security guard or policeman to live in the home. The guard may have lived in what was the maid's room (her name was "Annie") off the kitchen until the home was finally sold to the Pillarisettis.

Amarjit ("Amy") and Sudha Pillarisetti are the proud current owners of the Bolton home, the first residents after James C. and Fran Bolton. Both Pillarisettis are natives of India; Amy was born near Shimla in northern India while Sudha was born in Vizag in southern India. Both met while furthering their education in Chandigarh. Sudha became a surgical pathologist by profession while Amy chose a similar course in immunology. After marrying in London, they immigrated to the United States and lived in several cities early in their marriage before finally settling on Alexandria in 1989 for Sudha's employment.

One day, Amy drove by the then-long empty Bolton House and saw it was for sale. The home quite impressed her and after inquiring about the home, Sudha and Amy bought it in 1990. The house needed much updating and the Pillarisettis have made this magnificent two-story house both modernized and a home to enjoy and to be proud of.

One of the major changes that they made in the house was the remodeling of the kitchen area. The kitchen was small and still had the bells hanging that the Boltons used to "ring" for the maid to come and serve them elsewhere in the house. The home is now considered a landmark in the Alexandria community and sits on an elevated terrace portion of land that is partially surrounded by the First Methodist Church. Bayou Robert crosses the front of their home, requiring that they use a small bridge as part of their driveway. Supposedly in the house's very early years before the extensive growth of trees in the neighborhood, one could stand at Bolton House's front door and see all the way to the downtown area, specifically to the doors of St. James Episcopal Church on Bolton Avenue.

According to Sudha Pillarisetti, "What my neighbor, (Dr.) Milton Rhea, that sometime when they were building the house early on or they were excavating, a skeleton popped up. And the Smithsonian (Institute in Washington DC) guys came in and took it away. So the question is, was there an American Indian burial site here?"

Regarding the spirits that inhabit the Bolton/Pillarisetti home, Amy said, "When we bought the house, you know how it is when people put ideas about old houses. . . . In the beginning (of our moving in), I would hear footsteps in the attic. . . . Everyone (in my family) would laugh when they heard this. . . . Once someone else in the family, our son Anoop, said 'Well mom, I heard it (the footsteps) too.' So I feel like someone is walking up there . . . in the attic." Sudha said, "We have heard it quite a few times. She would say, 'I heard someone else walking up there.' And I would say it's an old house and it is just creaking and squeaking, you know." When asked of Amy what she thinks it really is, she said, "I just don't know. I thought it is probably Mrs. (Fran Sample) Bolton as she lived here for so long in this house. And maybe she comes to check it out. (She is checking to see that) The people who are living here (in this case, the Pillarisettis) are taking care of her house. If I were living in this house for thirty-five years and I would go away, I might come back also to see what was going on (like Mrs. Bolton). . . . I might come back to see if everything was okay and good. . . . I started hearing this right when we first moved in, 1991 or 1992. . . . I heard it for the first four or five years. . . . I think she (Mrs. Bolton) became satisfied that we were good people and she decided to leave and go free herself from this universal idiosyncrasy and go and rest completely.

"One day, this is crazy, I went up (in the attic) and found my attic was all moved around, things were all moved around. . . . Like I have set up my bookshelf (and I know exactly where everything was put), so if somebody has moved the stuff, I know it was moved. It may not be big stuff, but I will know for sure someone has moved it. So I went up there and said to myself, 'My attic didn't look like this!' But I just didn't think much of that at the time. . . . I go up in the attic all the time.

"When we cleaned the attic, we found all sorts of old photos of the Boltons. I took them to the school (Bolton High School) and gave them. The pictures were of the Boltons and of Bolton High School. My son (Anoop) did a study on the Boltons, and we have a copy of the report."

Ghosts come and go at times of their choosing at the Bolton House, but it is how they interact with their fellow inhabits of the dwelling that tells us so much!

# Pineville's Spirited Sites

# Tyrone Plantation

## "The Civil War Has Not Ended Here"

Tyrone Plantation house, located at 6576 Bayou Rapides Road outside of Alexandria, was built in 1843 by General George Mason Graham (1807-1891), a Virginian who came to Louisiana and fell in love with this state. Graham was raised in Virginia at Gunston Hall Plantation; his father was the secretary of war under two presidents, and his family members were friends and neighbors to the first five presidents of the United States. Graham was familiar with plantation life and built just outside of Alexandria a three storied house, a granary, a brick kiln, a sawmill, a cotton gin, and a wharf for barge traffic on the bayou. Graham wrote an autobiography and left much correspondence that is housed in various federal, state, and university archives. Graham also built what is probably the only underground tomb on a plantation in Louisiana and buried there his wife and a son. This has given rise to the story of the "soldier ghost" still living on the plantation.

Prominent on both a state and local level, Graham was named in 1856 as vice chairman, along with the governor of Louisiana as the chairman, of the Board of Trustees entrusted with the establishment of a state university for Louisiana. As it so happened, both Graham and the governor at the time, Governor James Madison Wells (1808-1899) were from Rapides Parish, and so, not surprisingly, the school was established in Rapides and was named the Louisiana State Seminary of Military Learning. Graham was responsible for everything in developing the school, from hiring the architect, to writing the school's charter, to hiring the faculty. And it was all done in Graham's personal study at the Tyrone Plantation home.

Graham hired future general William Tecumseh Sherman (1820-1891) as the first superintendent of the school. Sherman was a regular guest at Tyrone. But the onslaught of the Civil War took Sherman away and he never returned to serve again as superintendent of the school.

Graham served on the school's board for thirty years and is often referred to as the "father of LSU." The ownership of Tyrone eventually passed in 1915 to Mr. Charles Edward Robinson, the owner of a lumber mill in Boyce. Robinson made extensive repairs and alterations to Tyrone and modernized the upper two floors, discontinuing use of the brick first floor as the main living area. Mr. Arthur Robinson and his wife Amy, a granddaughter of George Mason Graham, were the second generation of Robinsons to live at Tyrone, but they moved to Alexandria upon the tragic death of their only child, whose sad laughter continues to be heard at Tyrone today. Tyrone was sadly neglected until it became a home again, this time to Colonel Rae A. Donaldson (1913-1994) and Marion Blanchard Donaldson (1920-2003). Their daughter, retired Judge Rae Swent, is the present owner. The Donaldson family operated Tyrone as a bed and breakfast for twenty-five years and family weddings have given way to those of friends and neighbors and now to the many happy brides from all over Cenla.

*Tyrone Plantation*

Retired Judge Rae Donaldson Swent is the owner of Tyrone now. One of the most respected people in North Louisiana, she is a petite woman but also very powerful. Longtime district judge of the 9th Judicial District Court, she is also one of the most respected historical preservationists, not only known statewide, but nationally too! And she is also a delight and fun to be with. She is the "great lady" of Tyrone and is just full of fascinating stories. Sitting on the lovely veranda front porch of Tyrone, here is what Judge Swent says about Tyrone's spirited world:

I did not understand it at the time, but in fact the very first night I spent here at Tyrone I heard the 'children ghosts.' That's what I call them, the children ghosts. My dad, his last (military) station was in Virginia. He was finally coming home. He bought this house in '54. In '61 was when he retired, so they had owned the house for some time (without ever having lived in the house) and my brother then was a student at LSU in Baton Rouge. I was visiting here (Alexandria) with relatives and he and I came out to the house the night before they arrived. I came out here with three of my sisters and we all decided to spend the night at Tyrone. There were beds, there were curtains, there was lots of stuff. This was stuff left over from prior owners, including Mr. Edward Robinson. His son married the granddaughter of George Mason Graham, the man who built the house. They had one child, and the child was playing on the porch (what is considered the second story or main floor of Tyrone) and fell off the porch and broke her neck. The young Robinsons left the house and rented it out for almost twenty years. The child died in the '30s. I do not remember her name at this time. Mr. Robinson, the elder, bought the house in 1912. His son, Arthur Robinson, remained here when the elder Robinson went back to Ohio. Arthur was a lawyer here in town (Alexandria) and he happened to marry the granddaughter of George Mason Graham. That is how he happened to know about the house.

They lived here until the child died. And then they moved out. I only met her (Mrs. Arthur Robinson) once. She came to the house one time after she moved out after my parents had moved in. She never set foot in the house again. . . .

My brother and I, we decided to come here and be here when mom and dad arrived (from Virginia). I was sleeping, in fact the room that I still sleep in now (located) on the second floor in the back. And I was woken up in the middle of the night by children laughing and playing. It sounded like a serious game of tag. Yeah, in the middle of the night. I looked out of my window and couldn't see anybody there, so I wondered if they had gotten into the first floor (the ground floor). There were a lot of children playing. I heard male and female voices just yelling, "Hah, Hah, Hah," I said (very expressively by Judge Swent) kind of thing. So I went upstairs to wake and tell my brother. They (the spirits) may have gone down to the first floor because I hollered out of the window, "What cha doing?" He went downstairs and came back and said that there was no one down there. Well, they must have run off and gone home, I thought. I didn't know for ten years until I had two ladies doing bed and breakfast here and they told me at breakfast, "Why were those children running around the porch laughing and playing?" I knew right away it was the same children that I had heard years before. The two ladies got up out of bed and came up here, and they found no one here. Same group of children like I said. Then I realized that I had actually heard the children ghosts. That is what we call them here. I had one other lady, another bed and breakfast guest, who actually heard the children also. She heard them outside and they also woke her up. When I heard the sound, it was definitely coming from the backyard. When the first two ladies heard it, the sound was coming from the porch. You can clearly hear (footsteps). And the other lady heard the children on the (right) the house and she told me the same thing. The children woke her up. She looked out of the window and there was no one there. For me, the duration lasted about ten minutes of laughing and playing before I decided, "Wait a minute, why are they in my yard? There are no children around here." I think she was only about five years old when she fell from the porch. . . .

Regarding the children, I cannot say how old they were. Their voices were high pitched. The male voices were maybe ten or twelve years old. So it could have been siblings playing, but she didn't have any siblings. But she might have had friends that came over to play. I mean, what do I know. I just know that I clearly heard children playing. And so did the ladies hear children playing. And they were positive. I was very surprised to hear children playing, what I now believe were ghosts. How could they be there?

**WRITER'S NOTE:** Upon my further historical research, it was actually the great granddaughter of General George Mason Graham who married Arthur Robinson. General George Mason Graham, 1807-1891, married Mary Eliza Wilkinson, 1830-1855, and had four children, the youngest being Amy Blanchard Graham, 1853-1940. Amy married General David Theophilus Stafford, 1849-1926, and they had twelve children. The oldest child, Dr. George Mason Graham Stafford, 1876-1958, married Virginia Curtis Cullen, 1878-1930, and they had five children, the oldest being Amy Graham Stafford, 1902-1982. Amy Graham Stafford married James Arthur Robinson, 1903-1972, in 1930. Their only child, the great, great granddaughter of General George Mason Graham, was Virginia Cullen Robinson, 1931-January 30, 1937. Virginia died on a Saturday night at 7:10 p.m. at Tyrone. She is described in her obituary as "An exceptionally bright and intelligent little girl for her years. . . ." She is buried at Mount Olivet Cemetery with her parents in Pineville.

> Our other ghost story, which is far more prevalent: I have had fifteen people tell me about our soldier ghost here. The first people to tell me about it were my first two grandchildren. When Hunter Swent was five and Jansen was two, they were playing downstairs and the adults were upstairs in the dining room. That was about 2007ish. That was before we were doing bed and breakfast. I had never heard anything like this before. Hunter came up the front stairs into the house. So, she (Jansen) came upstairs and said, "The man downstairs, he is pretty. He has a uniform." She has seen pictures of military people as I have some. And that is what she noticed about him. She recognized that he had on a military uniform, but she said it was a p-r-e-t-t-y uniform. So I said, "Well, let's go see who it is." So we walked downstairs and my grandson was just standing there looking at the door that we came in from and I said, "Well, did you see somebody down here?" He said, "Oh, yes, a soldier, I saw him, but he left." He said that they were in one room, came out into the middle room. The soldier came out of the other door (of the other room on the ground floor). And the soldier walked outside and was gone. So we didn't see anything by the time we got there.
>
> I asked them what color was his uniform. Hunter said, being so young, said that the uniform was "dark." She couldn't say because there was not a lot of light down there. It was either gray (likely for the Confederacy) or dark blue (likely for the Union). So she didn't say anything about that. But that was the first two people to ever tell me they saw a soldier down there.
>
> Now while my parents were alive, we did not use the first floor as a real living space. It was then the basement and my dad used it for storage. He had a desk in one of the rooms which he used to get away from everybody. A "man cave" of sorts. But it wasn't until dad died (in 1994). I told mom, "Let's improve downstairs (the ground floor). We can use this place as a bed and breakfast." It is truly a wonderful place. I was born with history in my head. My dad was not. He said, "Let's not spend money we don't need

to spend." (laugh) That was his attitude. So mother and I actually are the ones that did the historic effort, the effort to reestablish the historic character of the house. Mr. (Arthur) Robinson made some substantial changes (mainly adding a front room to where the other side of the front porch gallery was) like that room (pointing to the newer front room). So we decided to do that (reestablish the historic character of the house). It was a year long effort to find the right men to restore the house, but we had fun doing that. . . .

Going back to the soldier: We had at least fifteen people of those that came here over a ten year period that would simply come up to breakfast and say something like, "Who the heck was that guy wandering around?" Or they would say, "There was a very handsome gentleman here last night. We were very apologetic that we were there. He simply didn't say much and he just left." The women who saw the soldier were a lot more graphic in what they saw. Some would say though, "It was a blue uniform," or would say "It was a gray uniform." It definitely was not described as a modern uniform. But it was one they seemed to recognize. And I guess they simply associated the uniform with the age of the house. I just don't know. They came to the conclusion that the uniform was very old. Some would say the uniform has a lot of buttons. (laughing) I do remember one woman saying that. She said she believed it was blue and had two rows of buttons down the front and his pants were a different color. So everybody would have their own perception on something that they saw for two or three minutes.

Regarding when the last time that the soldier was seen, I haven't had any bed and breakfast customers since before the pandemic, since COVID, so I haven't had anybody down here to see the spirit of the soldier. Everybody who saw him back then said he did the exact same thing. He would come out of the same room downstairs each time. (If one is facing the front of the house, this room is on the right front on the ground floor.) They always say that he came out from there (that bedroom), stepped out of there and then looked around at everything.

I do have an opinion as to who it is. George Mason Graham had three sons. One was a prisoner of war at a Confederate prison in Georgia (Andersonville?) And when the war was over, he was transported to New Orleans because he was very malnourished and unhealthy. Now there is a famous architect in New Orleans by the last name of Freret (William Freret). He was transported to Freret's home because Freret was an excellent friend with George Mason Graham. Freret is the one that Graham had repaired (built?) the building that became the Louisiana State Seminary for Military Learning (the predecessor to Louisiana State University). He got Freret to come up here to fix what the first architect messed up (in building the Seminary building). And he put the four towers on the building that burned in 1869 that is just like the old state capitol building in Baton Rouge has. I have a lovely picture of it downstairs (ground floor) The boy had known where Freret lived (having visited there with his father previously) and he asked the people take there. And his father (George Mason Graham) came down from Alexandria to New Orleans to pick him up and bring him home. But in fact he died before he got home.

His body was brought home by his father. I understand that it took two weeks to travel to New Orleans by boat from Alexandria back then. The boy's body was displayed (as was the tradition of that time) in the front bedroom (of Tyrone) which was a bedroom at one time. I believe that he was the one that was buried in the (underground) tomb which I haven't fully excavated yet. Once, I paid this guy who had a GPR (Ground Penetrating Radar) to locate the tomb which is made of bricks. You shouldn't have difficulty finding it with GPR. Even though he couldn't find it, let me tell you how many times that I was in it over the years. Daddy showed it to my sister and I when we were too young to make sure we knew what it was. But when he showed it to us, I was very much preoccupied with family and did not memorize where it was. When I brought my four children from Houston to live here at Tyrone, my dad did not want my children to be playing in the crypt. He felt it was too old for children to be playing in there. So he filled up the staircase with dirt because it was an underground staircase. You would walk down, then turn, and there was a room. The man who came (with the GPR) did identify three graves in front of the (underground) tomb and (George Mason) Graham had built the tomb and put his son there so that he would be close to his mother. She was originally buried there, but (the body) has since been moved to (Old Rapides Cemetery in) Pineville. . . .

It is my belief that if somebody in the (Graham) family is still hanging around, it was that boy. . . . When the ghost people (the LSP

> investigators) came and did the voice thing (detection), they said the ghost's name was John. (George Mason) Graham had a son named John, but I thought it was the older son (Donald George Graham) who died shortly after the war in New Orleans. But it could be either or both. But they got some noise from the room which makes me nervous. Fortunately, I don't sleep in that room anyway. The noise comes from the room which the soldier spirit always comes from. . . . I have kept a log on a piece of paper what the ghost say to the various guests here. . . .
>
> It is a wonderful house to live in. Everyone in my family has stories about it now.

This son of George Mason Graham who died in New Orleans shortly after the war was his first child, Donald George Graham, 1848-1866. According to the biography of Graham, *General George Mason Graham of Tyrone Plantation and His People* compiled by his grandson, George Mason Graham Stafford in 1947:

> Donald George Graham entered the Confederate army in 1864 at the age of sixteen and served until the close of the war. He was discharged in 1865, holding the rank of lieutenant at the time. He was ill from some sort of dysentery contracted in the army and never fully recovered from it. However, he entered the University of Virginia soon after returning home, but the following year, his condition became so serious that he left the university and attempted to reach home. He succeeded in getting as far as New Orleans and died there at the home of Mr. William Freret, an architect and personal friend of the family. Mr. Freret had been the supervising architect for the Louisiana State Seminary and a warm friendship sprang up between the two families. . . .

There are several surviving references to Donald's death including a newspaper obituary, a printed death notice and an entry in the family Bible. The Bible entry noted, "They buried him in the flower garden at 'Tyrone' besides his young mother who had been buried there previously."

The LSP investigators came for an investigative tour in 2020. The LSP report of their visit to Tyrone Plantation says in part:

Reported Activity: Sounds of children running and laughing on porch area, an apparition of a Confederate soldier walking through the downstairs area, footsteps heard on the stairwell.

Investigation: The investigation was attended by seven investigators: Jennifer, Elissa, Lori, Charles, Brian, Steve, and Brandon. We were also accompanied by two reporters from the *LSU Legacy* Magazine as well as a student working on her senior class project. We set up two DVR systems to cover two floors of the house and used EMF meters and voice recorders. After the set up, we split into two groups and moved to different sections of the house. Steve, Elissa, Lori, Brian and the two reporters were in the downstairs area using a ghost box and got the name Luke repeated several times. Unfortunately, due to the nature of the ghost box, we do not believe it is as always credible evidence and take it as more of a personal experience. With that being said, on another occasion, the other group was downstairs using the ghost box when one of them asked if this is where they had died, and the ghost box stopped on the Radio Maria station when it was saying the Rosary. Again, it's not credible evidence, but no doubt freaky. We were able to get a few EMF spikes while investigating the downstairs bedroom.

Summary: Unfortunately, we were not able to get any other physical evidence for our night. We did have a great time at a beautiful home, and we were able to hang out with some really nice people. We would like to thank Judge Rae Swent for allowing us into her home and look forward to making a return trip sometime in the future.

Tyrone Plantation is an amazing home full of history, stories, and tradition. It is one of the treasures of Louisiana. But if you ever have the opportunity to visit there, be prepared, as your "host" may not be Judge Swent alone. . . .

# Old Rapides Cemetery

## "They Lie in The Ground in Repose, But They Do Not Rest"

Many can debate as to what is the most haunted building in Central Louisiana. One can make excellent cases on various buildings based on the various types of spirits present there and their frequency of appearance. But few can dispute what is the most haunted parcel of ground in all of Central Louisiana: The Old Rapides Cemetery.

The Old Rapides Cemetery might be unique in all of Louisiana based upon its particular founding history. The earliest years, though, are a bit clouded as those records are lost. The Rapides Parish Courthouse was burned in May of 1864 by Union troops retreating from their Confederate pursuers. Even the records of the Catholic Church that survived a century of strife were burned in the Cathedral church's fire in 1895. So very few pertinent local records survive, but we do know some early history from outside sources.

By 1764, several families had settled the area that would soon make up what became the Poste du Rapides, the area where the Old Rapides Cemetery lies. Sometime between 1774 and 1798, the ground where the Old Rapides Cemetery was begun to be used as a public burying ground. By the early 1800s, this tract of land which overlooks the Red River was frequently mentioned in surviving legal documents as a cemetery, then known as the "Old Catholic Cemetery."

The earliest surviving monument is that of Pierre Baillio who died at age fifteen in 1809. The tombstone survives in a cluster of elegant Baillio tombstones because all were imported marble and were well-built, above ground tombstones.

The cemetery itself sits on a bluff overlooking not only the Red River but also the larger city of Alexandria (in comparison to Pineville where the cemetery lays). Its location is not by happenchance. Spring flooding of the Red River was routine then. Both housing and farming land were frequently damaged by the inundating waters. Out of religious respect for the dead, this land that was designated for the cemetery was the choicest land available to have, being near impossible to flood. Yet, the land was hilly and had clear evidence of rocks making it less desirable for farming use.

The first Spanish commandant to live here at what became the Poste du Rapides was Etienne Marafret Layssard (1704-1790). Arriving here from the Illinois Poste in 1766, Layssard originally came here to build a tar works, an enterprise which would later fail. (Tar was used as a sealer for boats.) Layssard's tract of land, also high in elevation, was adjacent to the cemetery land and was used as a place to conduct the official business of Spain. Layssard was designated as commandant of the area in 1770.

Looking at the cemetery, one finds it totally random in the organization of grave sites. It is clear there was never an organization plan, or at best any organization planned was totally ignored. There is no rhyme or reason to the tombstone locations or to their directions. Likely the land was always considered to be of public use and each and every burial site was selected by the surviving family members with little or no consideration to any nearby older grave. Newer graves sit next to ancient graves. Tombstones of every sort exist. Elaborate fenced in family plots sit next to long abandoned tombs.

If there ever was a cemetery planned and created to be a movie prop for a horror movie, this cemetery would clearly be a role model. The road pathway, barely big enough for a model car, let alone a big truck, winds around the cemetery as a last-minute thought. There are many spots in the cemetery so isolated and blocked by graves that it is impossible now to get a grave digging machine in to dig a grave. But the old way of hand-digging a grave still does exist.

*The Old Rapides Cemetery*

A large overhanging hedge surrounds three sides of the graveyard giving the graveyard the peace and quiet it deserves. Without looking at the dead-end street which parallels the front fence, one would not realize that we are in the oldest section of downtown Pineville. Not only is this cemetery here, but this area is now designated by the Pineville City Council as part of the "Cemetery District," a designation unique in Louisiana. Within two blocks of Old Rapides Cemetery are six or seven cemeteries (depending on how you count them), all themselves historic and notable, but not as historic and notable as Old Rapides. Nearby Mt. Olivet Cemetery has its own buried Louisiana governor, Thomas Overton Moore (1804-1876).

But Old Rapides has Louisiana governor, James Madison Wells Sr. (1808-1899), the man who gave birth to public education in Louisiana and was the leader in the movement to honor President Andrew Jackson with a statute still gracing Jackson Square in the French Quarter in New Orleans. Old Rapides has so many superlatives in their permanent residents: Civil War soldiers from both sides, political and governmental leaders, founders of local towns, civic and business leaders, the founder of Louisiana State University, and many more. But the cemetery also has common folk, those that were important in their time, from brick layers to doctors to children dying of childhood ailments. Unlike so many other cemeteries, including cemeteries that exist today, Old Rapides Cemetery is not exclusively of one race. Though mostly white residents are found buried there as they could afford the cost of a tombstone in the early years, African Americans and mixed-race people are found there too. Old Rapides Cemetery reflects Main Street and the rural community well.

But don't be mistaken, everyone that is buried at Old Rapides did not die a normal death. Some were tragic, many were violent, and all were painful and sad. Each had a story to tell, if one is willing to hear it. Early deaths were often due to malaria, yellow fever, typhus, cholera and so many other diseases and ailments. The Mead family, with their magnificent obelisk which reaches high in the sky, lost five of their six children within a few years, with their mother soon following, dying of sorrow. And then there is the infamous case of Miriam Ravencamp Hyams who was crushed and drowned by the collision of two steamboats on one foggy night in the Red River in 1844. The daughter of a former lieutenant governor of Louisiana, her handsome tombstone tells the tale of her death, but not of her life. Another permanent cemetery resident, John Frost, was a victim of violence. He was killed in a duel in 1851 only days before his wedding. Every death, regardless of cause, left many mourners behind. Frost left a would-be wife, now a widow, at the altar.

*Various graves at Old Rapides Cemetery*

So one can easily understand why the spirits roam rampantly through this strange graveyard. (Another chapter in this book tells the tale of the strange happenings at the grave of the last Civil War soldier that was ever buried, buried now at Old Rapides.)

Reports from the many visitors from around the world who have come and paid their respects at the cemetery reveal that many visitors leave with having experienced something, something unusual at this unique cemetery. Some visitors just feel a vague presence of a sort, a presence that is nearly impossible to describe. They say they feel something warm or moist on cold days; others say they have felt a cold "touch" on warm days. Others in turn did not feel a presence but just felt anxious or just unexpectedly ill at ease. There was just something there that made the skin crawl, but nothing was actually there. Many a visitor leaves the cemetery quickly and refuses to ever return.

I decided to conduct a small experiment one night. At 11:00 p.m. one cool fall night, while the people of the City of Pineville were quickly settling down to a rest, while the traffic of nearby Main Street was almost nonexistent, I drove to the cemetery and entered it and took a walk to see what, if anything would happen. Once I entered the main gate, the surroundings quickly became dark and murky, the darkness that only a deep forest could provide. Only a few rays of light from a couple of faraway streetlights provided just enough light to identify where I was at, that is, a cemetery. The tombstones and grounds did indeed look very different from the hundreds of times that I had seen them during the day. As there was much more darkness than light now, I had to look carefully at the tombstones near my feet and try to read them in hopes that I might recognize the area where I was standing. I did bring a flashlight and only briefly turned it on when I bumped into anything, but otherwise I relied on my gentle walk and hoped a small ray of light would shine through.

What did I feel? Not really sure. I was admittedly fearful in general as it is known that there were occasionally homeless people who slept in the cemetery. But I didn't feel any clear definable spiritual contacts. Maybe I was forcing the issue. The stories of spiritual contacts were always about the visitor who was not expecting them. I not only was expecting them, I was *hoping* for them. But I will say of my short visit to the deeply dark and quiet cemetery that I did not feel at all relaxed. I felt something, something I just cannot describe, something heavy and tangible, but not definable. It was a feeling that I did not want to feel again.

What the permanent residents of this cemetery want and how they interact with the visitors there varies with the visitor and the visit. The permanent residents, though, are clearly in charge, not the visitors. Everyone that I have talked to over the years who has visited there experiences an unusual feeling while there and they seem to have a completely different individual experience from all others. Many though claim that they experience nothing, won't admit to others to have experienced anything. On the other hand, there might be some who claim to have an experience that might not be true.

But in any case, there is something that is going on at Old Rapides Cemetery. Something is reminding visitors that the permanent residents might at times be unhappy, or curious, or even lonely.

I recommend that if you choose to visit the cemetery, don't expect to have an otherworldly experience, but simply be open to it. And don't go alone, or at night either. Call me up and I will go with you and give you an insider's tour.

# THE UNKNOWN CIVIL WAR SOLDIER

## "ETERNAL REST HAS FINALLY COME"

There were many battles during the Civil War, with many important ones occurring in Louisiana. We all know of the major battles of the war, such as the First Battle of Bull Run, the Battle for Shiloh, the Battle for Antietam, the Battle for Gettysburg, and the Vicksburg Campaign, just to name a few. So many battles, so many deaths, so many bodies resting below hallowed Louisiana ground. But there were many lesser battles also, most usually called skirmishes, in which soldiers on both sides fought, and fought hard, and both often lost their lives too. They were often buried in graves where they fell, almost always unmarked, far from their own homes, families, and friends. These fallen soldiers were never seen again, their family and friends unable to ever pay their respects to them, not even knowing where their beloved young soldier would now lay for an eternity. And these soldiers were eventually forgotten, including the sites where they were buried. Each soldier and their death has a unique story, but only one strange story will be told here, a story that took over a century and a half to complete. This story is about the all so very short life, and quick death of an unknown Civil War soldier who became the very last military man buried of this ancient war.

The Louisiana Highway 1 state bridge, located at the intersection with Louisiana Highway 490, a bridge that crosses the beautiful Cane River located between Rapides and Natchitoches Parishes, was the scene of the Battle of Monett's Ferry. This site is completely rural even to this day and is mostly farmland and pasture countryside with only a rare vehicle ever passing through. There used to be a historical marker here denoting the battle, but just like the unknown soldier that laid here long awaiting and finally receiving his final burial, the marker was removed about a decade ago. The old marker, highlighted with Civil War era flags, was strangely sold to an unknown local buyer via the internet in 2023. In this time of often revisionist history, old markers and thinking make way for new thinking, usually now placing historical events in proper twenty-first-century contact. But we do know what the marker used to tell passers-by about this mostly forgotten battle:

Battle of Monett's Ferry
April 23, 1864

> On this site was fought one of the critical engagements of the Red River campaign. After Mansfield, the retreating Federal Army under General N. P. Banks headed for Alexandria, pursued a smaller Confederate army under General Richard Taylor. Taylor devised a daring plan to encircle the Federals and cut off their lines of retreat. Gen. H. P. Bee was to hold the vital crossing at Cane River, occupying a position on the bluffs south of the river. Bee repelled an attack by the troops under Gen. W. H. Emory, but hearing that his flanks were turned he withdrew, thus permitting the Federals to continue to Alexandria.

People have long scoured this hallowed site for war souvenirs, probably as far back as since the war ended. But current legend has it that there is much more going on here than just souvenir hunters scrounging for the remnants of war. Legend has long had it that the spirits of the fallen walk the area purportedly looking for their fellow soldiers. Vehicles often stall here when they have to pass through the battle site. Is this the way the long-lost soldiers still call attention to the battle and themselves? Or are they angry that their lives and their deaths have been long forgotten?

One such soldier that haunted this battle site for a century and a half is now finally resting at peace. His name remains unknown, but his memory is now resurrected and honored. Here is his incredible story:

On November 10, 2010, a farmer plowing his harvested field on the battlefield of the Battle of Monett's Ferry uncovered what appeared to be a human bone. He immediately reported this to the Natchitoches Parish Sheriff's office as the site of the bone lays just on the Natchitoches Parish side of Cane River. The initial investigation by the sheriff's office and coroner determined that there was an entire human body buried there, though some damage occurred due to the plow. But the body was completely decomposed and all that was left was the skeleton. But how long was it lying there? Famed forensic anthropologist and author Mary Manheim from Louisiana State University in Baton Rouge Forensic Anthropology and Computer Enhancement (FACES) Laboratory was called to the scene. Who was this deceased person, how long has he been there, why was he buried in a field and, most importantly, how was he murdered?

The body was only buried just inches below the surface and was almost completely intact. Even most of his teeth were found there. Missing, strangely, was just the corpse's feet. The body was found lying on his back with both his legs and left arm laying at his side. His right arm, though, was found raised over his head. The skeleton was found to be bleached, completely dry, and was devoid of any odor of decomposition. The skeleton was declared by the anthropological team as being "historic" in nature, meaning it was a burial from a long time ago. But when?

Many artifacts were found with the body that partially told the corpse's story. Artifacts included buttons, made out of porcelain, metal, and possibly wood, a belt buckle, shoe "tacks," shoe or boot remnants, and, most importantly, bullet fragments. X-rays were taken of some of the vertebrae showing lead fragments in the bone, almost without a doubt being bullet fragments. All these items were compared with the items found on Civil War soldiers' bodies that were buried at the siege of Port Hudson, a major battle site located north of Baton Rouge, and all of these items were found to be consistent with them. Therefore, this was a deceased Civil War soldier from the battle of Battle of Monett's Ferry. But who was he?

Nothing was found that fully identified the body, not even as to what side, Confederate or Union, he fought on. And from this point, the investigation of who this body was stalled.

The remains of the body and artifacts were moved and stored carefully with the Louisiana Division of Archaeology and there they remained in a dark wooden box for nearly eleven years, almost forgotten about. The director of the division, Dr. Chip McGimsey, knowing of my interest as a Central Louisiana historian and my respect of matters of this nature, tasked me with the great challenge: to bury the soldier's remains with due military honors, but without providing any needed financial resources.

With the conviction of honoring this unknown deceased soldier who gave up his life for his beliefs and his country, I planned and implemented an elaborate, but most appropriate funeral for the last Civil War soldier expected to be ever buried, almost 170 years after the end of the war. But where would there be an appropriate plot of local ground available that also contained the remains of other Civil War soldiers? Well, there was only one place that met this description, a place, coincidently, possibly considered to be the most haunted site in all of Central, if not North Louisiana, a place revered with nearly 250 years of fascinating history. And that most resounding burial place was Old Rapides Cemetery, located in Pineville, Louisiana.

Now owned by the City of Pineville, this historic graveyard is both magnificent and very haunted. (See the chapter on the Old Rapides Cemetery) This cemetery was appropriate for this much belated soldier's burial for many reasons, but most importantly because other Civil War soldiers, Union and Confederate, are buried here. If it is true that there is any kinship among the deceased, one can only imagine the stories told to each other among the long deceased soldiers now buried here: Who was more gallant, heroic, tactically brilliant, and who was tragically killed. Were these long-forgotten soldiers now of the earth expecting another comrade to come rest with them, or was it a surprise to them after 170 years? There have been numerous stories passed down by the twenty-three generations of people who have trodden upon the cemetery's grounds, of their seeing strange sights here, hearing strange sounds, and feeling a strange tension as though one is not alone in spirit. This cemetery is an underground city filled with the leading citizens not only of the Central Louisiana area but also of the state and nation. Along with military leaders, societal leaders, and political leaders, including a nineteenth-century Louisiana governor, there lays here a Spanish commandant who ruled the area when Louisiana was owned by Spain. The stories that could be told also of violent and tragic deaths, deaths that were so shocking that even if one did not believe in ghosts, one would still wonder if a spirit of the victims of violence deserved their own eternal vigil of the afterlife. On many layers, this long-lost soldier is finally finding a home befit of his life and of his death.

After months of planning, the gathering of the money to finance the burial, and trying to find mourners who would share the loss and would want to pay their respects, a full-fledged memorial and funeral service was set up for February 18, 2022. The funeral director, Graham Kramer, who had prepared the bones and remnants chose to encase the remains as well as relevant paperwork in a water and airtight coffin. Although one would hope that the bones of the deceased will finally be left alone for all of eternity, the future is yet to be written on what mankind would do upon finding this well-sealed coffin. The Knights of Columbus Fourth Degree Color Corp Honor Guard from the Monsignor Piegard Council #1135 carried the coffin to the grave while local military veterans provided additional pomp and ceremony in the style of a fallen hero. As the deceased soldier is not recognized as to whether he was on the Union or Confederate side, he was honored in his giving of his life for a cause unknown. Along with Catholic priests (Father Anthony "Raj" Dharmaraj and Father Tom Kennedy) who oversaw the religious aspects, I gave the moving eulogy, a eulogy for a hero. As I said in the eulogy:

> One soldier, be it Union of Confederate, we do not know, was fatally wounded by a miniball, the ammunition of that time, and was buried in shallow soil. He was a beloved son to his parents, a loving brother to his siblings, and a cherished one to his wife or fiancé. But his name has been sadly lost to the passage of time and this unknown soldier's remains had laid restfully in our native soil for 147 years until his remains were accidentally disturbed and recovered in 2010.
>
> Now, this unknown soldier is finally returning to the earth and to his permanent rest. It is our duty and obligation to give him the peace that he and everyone so richly deserves at the time of their passing. . . .

*The unknown soldier's funeral on February 18, 2022*

Now the soldier finally lies deep and quiet in the dark earth, marked only by a granite marker proclaiming him as the unknown soldier of the Civil War, the last to obtain eternal rest. People, for various personal reasons, nowadays often come to visit his grave, all wondering who he was, what he had done, where he was from, how he felt at the moment of his death and why he was forgotten about for so long a time. But alas, here is the rub, as Shakespeare once said. Many who visit this now immortalized soldier's resting spot have told me and others that when they were there at the grave site, they have felt an eerie presence, a presence of someone who was with them though they were usually all alone. Although this cemetery is filled with the roaming, lost spirits of long-forgotten people, this one spot, this one very spot, often attracts the most allegiance, concern, and attention among those who are fearful of spirits. Is this fallen soldier the one who stands with those who come to pay their respects? Is he vengeful or playful? What is his goal in making his presence known?

Visitors to the grave testify in sincerity to what they feel. Sometimes they feel a wind on a windless day. Others feel like there is a heavy feeling—humidity on an otherwise dry day. Still others feel something inward, a near indescribable presence, something that only a person who has experienced it can understand. It doesn't happen to everyone, nor does it happen all the time. The feeling doesn't target just believers or nonbelievers, it just "happens" when one least expects it.

The feeling of being with spirits happened very surprisingly to me when I least expected it. I have visited the cemetery hundreds of times. As a dedicated volunteer for cemetery cleanup, I have washed, cleaned, and worked on seemingly most tombstones in every section of the cemetery, at one time or another. In fact, I have even discovered tombstones buried under dirt that were not previously known. Some of my visits over the decades have been of short duration, others all day, some for ceremonial activities and other visits for research purposes. But never have I truly felt a distinct presence until one late summer day in 2022.

Whenever I park my car off the cemetery property, I walk through the main entrance and would now routinely pass the unknown Civil War soldier's grave only yards off the road. Usually, I would walk over to it to make sure all was in order and well. This one particular hot and dry day, I walked over to the grave site expecting to do a quick and routine inspection. It was obvious upon arrival that there was no one in the cemetery since most people drive there and their cars would be parked within sight. Today, no cars, no people, and no activity whatsoever was evident. It was a quiet and peaceful day, but just very hot and dry as Louisiana summers can be.

When I walked up to the tombstone, I stood there to quickly survey it, and then I planned to leave moments later. I was usually there just long enough to read the brief inscription and remind myself why it was there. Then it hit me like being tackled; it felt like someone had wrapped their arms around me, a cold and moist skin next to my warm and dry skin. And as quickly as it happened, the feeling was gone almost completely. I nearly fell to the ground with both surprise as well as self-protection. Whirling my head around, I looked with wide-open eyes—no one was there. I looked all around; all was quiet. I quickly looked behind the closest large tombstones just in case the person who grabbed me had hid. No one was there. Nothing was around except tombstones, an endless array of tombstones. I stopped myself for a moment to think; what just happened? Did it really happen? Then I recalled the feeling of being grabbed and I knew I didn't make it up or dream it. It happened and it happened to me. *Me.* I immediately left the cemetery ignoring whatever I was there originally for. I did not tell anyone, until right now in writing, as who would believe me? It did happen and I will never forget it. I don't care what others think. I now know the apprehension of people wanting to tell of their own spiritual encounters.

*The unknown soldier's grave*

The questions are: Is this experience the unknown soldier, and was his act an act of his friendship or his disgust? I will never know. Since that visit, I have often returned to the cemetery, but usually now with someone else or a brief visit. Not that I am scared (maybe a little though), but maybe, just maybe, if it were to happen again to me, I would then maybe would have a witness.

Maybe it will happen again someday before I too become dust and maybe become a fellow spirit too.

# OLD PINEVILLE CITY HALL

## "ONE STOP-SHOPPING FOR A GUARANTEED HAUNTING"

Most places in Central Louisiana have a "welcoming" and pleasant appearance. Even haunted places, like some plantation homes, are beautiful in outward appearance and are quite inviting in outer design and setting. Few places, though, in Central Louisiana look as generally foreboding and rather unwelcoming as what is traditionally called the Old Pineville City Hall. Boxy and looming in appearance, its usual dirty outer look of old-fashioned art deco-style bricks, its broken front window, its old-style hanging balcony, and its most unattractive shrubbery lodged in front of the building remind one of their childhood where there was always this creepy, old abandoned house in one's neighborhood that no one seem to know what was inside and no one wanted to find out.

The "Old" (as most call it) Pineville City Hall is a dominating feature of the timid Pineville downtown. Sitting among a scattering of the old downtown businesses, it is reminiscent of an old, ignored guard dog sitting and waiting to be called. It is appropriate that the side street, Shamrock Street, leads directly into the Central Louisiana State Hospital, a (in)famous mental hospital of sorts, another very haunted site. The old city hall site is about ten blocks down Main Street from the Old Rapides Cemetery, another site of haunted happenings. But the Old Pineville City Hall is unique in all of Central Louisiana in its design, in its history, and of its current status of abandonment.

Designed by noted local architect C. Errol Barron Sr. in 1931, the city hall is unique in its design. The brick arrangement in this large two-

*Old Pineville City Hall*

story building, at first glance, clearly resembles the 1930s art deco-style. But upon closer examination, one must wonder what the architect really had in mind for his design model. Even the architect's aged son, C. Errol Barron Jr., also a noted architect, is unclear what message his father was trying to convey with the design. The building is two stories, but the stories reflect the prior age of ten-to-twelve-foot ceilings where the summer heat could gather in the days before air-conditioning. So, the building appears much taller and larger than a two-story building should in our time. If I had to guess what the building's purpose was without knowing beforehand, I would have to say that it looks like a very old prison, like the old DeRidder Gothic jail. But this building is much more complex, one of the most complicated buildings of its era in North Louisiana.

When it was built nearly a century ago as a city hall, it was made for "one stop-shopping" of a sort. Inside this hidden monster of a building, it originally housed the fire station, the police station, the tax department, the water department, the mayor's office, the city court, the judge's office, the city clerk, the city library and, most importantly, the city jail. As big as the building is, it is still hard to believe all these city offices were pigeonholed in this one compact building. It is a magnificently designed building and well deserving of its new national register status.

The doorway to enter this complex is in the center. The two old-style wooden doors are decorated in such a way that you might expect the doors to be the entrance to a castle, not a city hall. When entering this now-shuttered facility these days, the building is profoundly cold, dark, and slightly damp. You first enter a dark alcove that leads to a hallway ahead, and slightly to the right, the entrance of the first office. This hallway is the key to the entire building. At the end of the hallway, taking a left leads to the police and fire departments. Taking a right leads to what was the water and tax departments as well as the mayor's office. (The mayor had a secret side door where he could slip in and out of the building with no one knowing.) To the right-center of the building is also the old concrete staircase leading to the second floor. Not only is the staircase made of concrete, but one also slowly realizes that while walking through this building, the whole inside mostly appears to be poured or plastered concrete, almost like a gigantic concrete block. The inside is not inviting and reminds one of what the inside of old jails look like. This dominance of concrete gives the building's feeling of being cold and quite uninviting, that one shouldn't be in there.

As one trudges up the concrete staircase along the old metal railing, the staircase stops and turns in front of a large front window where one can look out at the very center of the old town of Pineville—the important intersection of Main and Shamrock Streets. One can see in the far distance the entrance to the National Cemetery, where beginning with the Civil War and the capture of Alexandria, the military dead are mostly resting. Unlike most any other city in Louisiana, downtown Pineville is like a city of the dead. More cemeteries are located on and slightly off Main Street than any other city in Louisiana, maybe the entire South. Even two Louisiana governors apparently choose to be buried here. One can easily determine that there are more dead people than alive that live in downtown Pineville. Even the Pineville City Council declared the area the first "Cemetery District" in the state of Louisiana. In fact, the people of the larger city of Alexandria located just across the Red River from Pineville used to have their deceased buried here, carried across on a ferry in the old timey days. So if one is looking for their ancient loved ones buried in Central Louisiana, come to Pineville first, and there is a good chance you will find them resting or otherwise. So, when one is looking out of this portrait window along the staircase of the Old Pineville City Hall, there is a good chance if you wait long enough that you may see a hearse going by with a new permanent non-voting resident for downtown Pineville.

After the wide staircase twists around going up, one finally arrives on the imposing second floor. The second floor is a bit reminiscent of the first, but it feels much better as it is well lit from the light from the staircase window which brightens the whole central area. In this wider second-floor hallway, one goes left to go to the courtroom which, at the far front end, at one time held bookshelves with books for the former city library. The courtroom itself is mostly plain but has many windows, making it a generally pleasant and well-lit place to visit. But at first, one might not notice a small door on the side of the judge's bench on the far-left side of the building. This door clearly goes toward the back of the building. Does it lead to the judge's personal office? Some other important room? No. It leads right to the city jail!

The jail is almost everything that you would want and expect of a haunted jail to look like, minus only the hanging chamber. The rooms are concrete, of course, with two brick walls and have heavily barred windows. The beds are hanging on iron platforms as one would expect from a century-old prison.

The cells are tiny; two small men stretching their arms out in a line would reach the long side walls of the cell. The feeling of being in it, especially when the door is closed, is like being sealed in a tomb. It is uncomfortable, dank, very, very cold in winter and very, very hot in summer. There is just nothing pleasant, to say the least, about being in there, which I suspect was part of the punishment. Added to that is that the outside of the three cells is a small hallway of similar construction which provides another layer of seclusion to anyone in the jail. Based upon the totality of construction materials in this area, likely someone screaming in the jail could not even be heard in the courtroom or anywhere else. If the City of Pineville had this abandoned ancient city hall, I suspect one would find there is no place more secluded than this jail in all of Central Louisiana.

From the second-floor hallway, if one goes toward the right side of the building, you enter one of the largest rooms of the building, an open-plan room that runs from the front of the building to the back. It is large in comparison to the other rooms of the building (though small by today's typical governmental standards) and may have been originally divided up into the judge's office and clerk's office. There are lots of windows though that could offer light, but the shades are all pulled down making it a room full of shadows with corners of darkness.

Back downstairs on the right side of the building, past the beginning of the staircase, is an open room with an old-time gigantic walk-in safe. This room was originally used for the city tax office and likely the water department was also housed in the room. On the farthest right side of the room is a tiny, short hallway that leads to the back of the building toward the equally small mayor's office. When you enter, one can see that the average size desk in there takes up almost one-third of the room! The room is in the back corner of the building, almost hidden (purposely?) from the public. There is a "secret" door off this tiny hallway that leads to the right-side exterior of the building that the mayor could slip in and out without anyone noticing.

When one enters the first floor, going to the left side of the building, you are entering the fire and police departments. The two rooms and side restroom are again tiny in comparison to today's standards, but I guess they were enough for the City of Pineville nearly a century ago. But what is most noteworthy of this section of the building is the large garage whose entrance takes up the front left side of the building, about half of the front. In it these days it holds a 1950s era, mostly restored fire truck and an early car made up to look like an old police car. This room is fun to be in, probably the only "fun" room in the building, as who doesn't like to see an old timey fire truck and police car!

The "new" Pineville city hall was built in 1974 and is located a bit farther down Main Street from the old city hall, so this old building suddenly became purposeless in 1974. It sat unused, I'm told, for almost fifteen years when a then dedicated group of the proverbial "little old ladies" convinced the mayor to turn the building into a city museum. And indeed, they did so quite successfully. In 1994, the building reopened as the only city hall museum in the state. Schoolchildren enjoyed seeing the old fire truck and police car and everyone else enjoyed the various exhibits, most of which were located on the second floor. But alas, after the initial excitement wore off and the little old ladies who voluntarily ran the museum started dying off, the doors were locked and the lights turned off. A window AC unit was allowed to continue running to reduce the overall humidity in the concrete building. The homemade exhibit displays quickly faded, and everything began to collect dust. A few very rare visitors over the years got a special tour from the then-current city administration, but otherwise the building was mostly quickly forgotten about and ignored. It got so bad for the old city hall that many of the citizens of Pineville didn't even realize they had an old city hall!

Fast forward the calendar to today, and several dedicated local historians and preservationists, including yours truly, began bringing attention to the museum. The application for National Registry status was approved. Restoration to selected portions of this slowly deteriorating building were begun under the current mayor of Pineville, Rich Dupree. At the time this book is developing, there is much hope for a revitalization and a second full restoration of the building to happen. We shall wait and see if our hopes are satisfied or dashed.

But what does this building have to do with spirits and ghosts you say? Well, try visiting this building late at night and you will see!

I had the opportunity over a twenty-four-hour period to go in the building to take pictures regarding beginning the process of the renovation. Well, I chose a time that probably no one in the last half of a century had chosen—to walk the halls and rooms of this abandoned building—at night! And even though I couldn't see well, touring the building in the dead of night was truly an eye-opening experience!

Driving up to the building on Main Street deep into the night, I first realized that the downtown streets, especially Main Street in front of the old city hall, were totally devoid of people and traffic. I think that I could have easily laid down in the middle of the street for a minute or two and would not have been bothered by any concern of being run over. Likewise, I saw no one walking the streets either. (My previous visit at night to the nearby Old Rapides Cemetery was a very similar experience of total quietness and seclusion.) The only noise that I could now hear that I didn't hear during the day was the clicking of the changing of the red light at the Main and Shamrock Street intersection. I could also hear the drone of light traffic traveling on Louisiana Highway 28, better known by the locales as "the expressway," which was several blocks away and mostly parallel to Main Street. Looking up and down Main Street, I saw the occasional change of the streetlight and various nighttime outdoor buildings' security lighting, but little more. Just as the downtown cemeteries in Pineville's "Cemetery District" were dead quiet, so was the center part of the City of Pineville after hours.

Walking up to the old city hall, I found that there were no lights anywhere nearby, so the closer one gets to the building, the darker it becomes. I'm glad that I brought a small flashlight that I planned to use only when I really needed to. Near the front door, I was soon totally engulfed in darkness and would not have been seen by anyone at the nearby intersection waiting for the light to change. Likely I was the first person to enter the building in a half century, or more, at night.

After carefully opening the outer glass protective door, I fumbled for the key and door lock and finally found both. I put the key near the old lock and jiggled it until I could find the right position for the key to go in. It was rather difficult as I could not see the key lock opening. As I was doing this, I started to feel very strange. Was I truly alone? I looked around and nothing had changed, other than the ever-changing red light. But I still felt as though I wasn't alone. It is true that the homeless (or "unhoused" as they are now called) population is ever growing and now seemingly everywhere, so I had to look around to make sure that one of these unfortunate people were not there with me also lost in the shadows. As my eyes got used to where I was standing, I saw no one else present, or at least visibly present. But I couldn't shake the feeling that I was not entirely alone.

As I turned the key, the lock resisted my efforts. Maybe it needed a bit of oil to be injected, or maybe I was just not wanted by the building. For the most part, the building had been left alone and had simply just sat there watching as the world revolved around it. But the lock finally gave way, and I could hear the bolt slide slowly in. I tugged on the door, and it released like a well-sealed refrigerator door. I made one last look around. All appeared to be dead quiet. I was alone, maybe. And then I entered.

The downstairs hallway next to the staircase was very dark, illuminated only by a couple of poorly placed streaks of light sneaking through the flag-covered staircase window. Fortunately, I was familiar with this room's set up and passageway, otherwise I would have turned around and quickly departed. The feeling of being in this passageway room was completely different from that of being outside or, quite frankly, anywhere else. Yes, it was cold, very cold, though the general weather was warm. The building was likely very difficult if not impossible to heat and the concrete and fixtures did not retain any of the heat from the daytime heating. It was cold, but a different sort of cold, a cold that embraces one as though you were being hugged, seeking and finding every small opening in your clothes to snake down into your skin and become a part of you. I don't think I could have worn enough coats to have warmed up. I just had to ignore the embracing cold and let it take over my body.

I looked up and around from where I was standing. I recognized the general features of the building, but the open area where I was standing which reached the top of the second floor felt as though I was in one of those massive tourist caves people visit with a few little guide lights sporadically placed at the bottom of the walls. There were no guide lights pointing up here, just rare unequal shafts of lights, likely coming from windows located in the other nearby rooms with the light bouncing around this room. It was truly like a kaleidoscope, but a dark foreboding kaleidoscope like I have never seen before. I didn't like what I saw, but even worse, what I felt was the embracing cold in a way like it was crushing me. I will just go ahead and say it, though it is hard for me to rationalize—I was not wanted there by the building or maybe the essence of the deceased people who had inhabited the building. It is not a pleasant feeling, kind of like I ate some bad food that settled very poorly in my stomach. I was feeling an onslaught of attacks against all my senses. I did not like this at all. It was a very real, very clear feeling. Something was definitely there. I also had that feeling when I drink way too much coffee and was over-caffeinated. I was anxious, queasy, and cold—all a bad combination. I tried to settle myself and take a few breaths. There was nothing visible there with me. It was just a building. It was just night. I was alone. I had to move on. If I didn't explore this place now, I would never explore this place or any other like it at night again. I must move forward!

The old city hall was quiet, exceedingly quiet. There was not a hint of a sound, not even from the droll of the constant traffic from the expressway. I could hear my breathing, louder than I expected. And I could feel my heart beating, a feeling I told my heart doctor that I never can feel. I cannot recall ever being so sensitive to all of my surroundings. So, without any planned thought, I moved forward. I was going to explore the building, including the jail. I didn't know if I was doing this for my book, or for myself. I was not a brave person, but at some point in one's life one has to try something different, a bit daring, and maybe be a little foolish.

As I previously said, I knew the general features of the building. I knew pretty surely that I wasn't going to step into a pit or a massive spider web. But I still felt the wall as I moved forward, getting what I believed was decades of dust and plaster on my fingers and palm. I planned to move forward quickly, mostly without thought, as a logical person would have long ago turned around and made their exit. I quickly climbed the stairs, more lit because of the proximity of the staircase window, but still very poorly lit. The steps seemed larger and higher than before when I ascended them during daylight. My sensitivity was high regarding my surroundings; I felt the movement of air around me. My steps on the staircase reverberated all around, like I was leading a parade. There was no sneaking through the building. Whatever was there had to know I was there now.

Soon I was on the second floor. I decided these feelings, which continued to grow, were reaching a peak. I was expecting a presence, human or otherwise, to grab my shoulder at some point. The presence would be the spiritual guard from the house or however one would call him or her. I started looking in every shadow corner and was more distressed not to find the guard there than to find him. At least if I found him, I know what to avoid or protect myself from. Not knowing where this spiritual guard was worse because I felt and I knew that I would find him when I least expected.

I quickly headed through the better lit courtroom toward the jail. The courtroom was big, and the shadows and sparse rays of outside lighting acted like a complicated spider web through the building. In some ways, I could see less than the darker area downstairs. The shadows and light tended to confuse whatever I was seeing. Was it an empty space or was it courtroom seating? Or was it something else? The courtroom felt no safer or more comfortable than anywhere else.

I tugged on the door leading to the jail area. It was stuck and rubbing the floor or something else that I have never experienced before there. What (or who) was holding the door? So with one last jerk, the door begrudgingly opened for me. What I peered into was the darkest area of the building. I knew the general structure of what the jail looked like during the day, and it didn't look like this. Yes, it was much darker back here. This was the back left corner of the building, far away from the few streetlights of Main Street. There was no outdoor lighting behind the building, only plant overgrowth dominating behind this ancient structure. But I made it here, for the first and certainly only time in my life. I was only feet away from the near century-year-old jail cell, full of the living memories of convicts whose stories are still being told as warnings to children. It was even colder here, like I was inside a freezer, but the colder feeling was not logical. Something was cold and lingering back here and was staring at me. I was staring at him and not seeing him, but kind of hoping that I would not see anything. Just a few more steps and then I could leave triumphantly, or at least alive.

Each final step that I took toward the paint-pealed jail cell, I tried to convince myself I was actually a step closer to leaving. My stomach was fully upset now, full of stomach acid working on undigested food or worse. My journey into this Dantesque place was almost over. Just a few more steps. I felt more alone than I ever had felt. The enveloping cold on my body was totally encasing. Two more steps. I was inside the door. I put my right hand behind me to make sure the door would not close on me or at least be warned that the door was closing. It was a deep dark in the corners of the cell, dark as though the corners had never experienced light. That's it. That's enough. I didn't need to test myself or the building's spirits anymore. I never expected to feel what I felt. It is truly unexplainable by me. Something was there and they were very unhappy with me. It was time to leave!

I turned and exited the cell with little thought, but quick movement. I was more interested in departing than anything around me anymore. By the time I made it to the staircase, I had started to feel better, less anxious, less pressure on me. My stomach was still queasy, but it wasn't getting worse, which was something good. I wanted to run down the staircase, but I could see myself tripping in the dark and falling and hitting my head or worse. Although I rushed down almost as cautious as I went up, I was still rushing down fast. It was finally over. Whatever I was feeling from this haunted house of a building was hopefully nearing an end. At the bottom I made a quick turn. My feet were loud everywhere in the sudden silence of this building. Once I hit the first floor, I rushed to the exit door, not looking back. I opened the door, pushed my way through the glass door and then started to walk away. I turned—the door needed to be locked. I again fumbled for the keys and lock, but the lock strangely cooperated this time. *Door locked!* I turned, took a breath, momentarily relaxed. It was over. All the strange and uncomfortable feelings that I felt in the building were either gone or rapidly leaving me. I was as before, just a man standing in the dark and shadows. No one on the streets still; the red light again turned green, green for go. *Where was my car, there,* I said out loud, surprising myself. It was truly over. I started my car, made a U-turn, and headed thankfully home.

What did I feel in that strange building? It was much more than fear or anticipation. The air was dense and cold around me. Supposedly, some have said, cold air means evil spirits. I don't know if that is true, but clearly I was surrounded by spirits who did not want me there. I was not a welcome visitor. No matter how much I explain to the reader, I cannot entirely explain what I felt or what I saw. I am glad I went there, but my visit there is much more appreciated as a past memory rather than a current event.

I don't know if the reader will have the opportunity to ever do what I was able to do. But if you do have the opportunity, *be forewarned!* This is not a joke or make believe. I felt something there, something alive, be it the building or spirits who reside in the building. Trespassers are not welcome, nor are people still living. . . .

# Spirited Sites Around Rapides Parish

# LOYD HALL

## "THE GHOST BEHIND THE WINDOW"

Of the great old plantation homes of Louisiana, few can rival the magnificent Loyd Hall (not "Loyd's Hall" as some may say) at 292 Loyd Bridge Road, Cheneyville, Louisiana. Its history is both glorious and mysterious, a rare combination for such a legendary and well-known building and estate.

Nestled quietly on a peaceful farming road just outside of the equally historic Lecompte, Louisiana, in Rapides Parish, the drive to the Loyd Hall estate through the small city of Lecompte is both a lovely and peaceful one, part of its charm. Though Loyd Hall is not a part of the city of Lecompte, Lecompte itself in many ways closely resembles the historic complexities of Loyd Hall itself.

Lecompte was originally called Smith's Landing after the legendary nineteenth-century character of Ralph Smith Smith. (That is his real name, 1806-1883). The history of Lecompte and the area really begins with him. In 1832, Smith, who had been a construction engineer on the B&O Railroad, came to the nearby town of Cheneyville and acquired a large plantation in that area. Growing successful crops was not a problem for Smith, a man of many talents, or any of the other local plantation owners in that area but getting the crops to the market was. Smith conceived of placing barges on the local navigable waterway called Bayou Boeuf to transport not only his crops but also, for a fee, the crops of his neighbors. But along with placing barges on the bayou, he decided to use his learned skills, talents, and contacts and build his own small railroad from this area that was soon to be named after him, Smith's Landing, all the way to the parish seat of Rapides Parish, Alexandria, located about fifteen miles away. Construction of the railroad began in 1832 and was completed in 1837. What makes this railroad so very important in our Central Louisiana history is that this railroad is universally believed to be the first railroad ever built west of the Mississippi River. The railroad's track was later demolished by the Union troops during the Civil War in order to build the uniquely fascinating Bailey's Dam on the Red River in Alexandria. But that is another story to tell for another time.

Lecompte's unique name comes from a completely different set of circumstances. Lecompte is named after a famous racehorse that was named LeComte who, in turn, was named after the well-respected nineteenth-century horse breeder and lover of horses, Ambrose LeComte. (When another railroad company came through Lecompte in the later 1800s and painted a sign for the town on the side of the train depot, a "p" was accidentally added to the name—and it has remained part of the town's name ever since.) LeComte the horse was most famous for winning the races at the Fair Grounds racetrack in New Orleans.

Leaving the city of Alexandria on US Highway 71 going south, a short ten-mile excursion to Lecompte, and passing the landmark Louisiana State University of Alexandria, gives one the feeling on how the countryside must have looked in centuries past that was surrounding Loyd Hall and how it must have felt living there 150 years ago and more. Sugarcane and cotton production, the enslaved peoples working the fields, beautiful homes, and commercial traffic on the Bayou Boeuf, all were the common sights to see then. Upon arriving in Lecompte, one sees the ever-popular and well-regarded Lea's Lunchroom, a must-stop eatery famous for its selection of culinary pies which made the city of Lecompte the "Pie Capitol" of the state. Famously founded by (Pryor) Lea Johnson Sr. (1896-1995), who once appeared on the Johnny Carson *Tonight Show* program on November 23, 1989, and famously bested old Johnny in a battle of who could be wittier.

One can then turn right into downtown Lecompte and drive through a cluster of ancient buildings and houses reflecting a different era, an era when your life was lived in your hometown, and no farther. One will pass on the right the summer home of former pre-Civil War governor, James Madison Wells (1808-1899), another home evoking thoughts of the hay day of the distant past. One continues the short drive on the tight one-lane highway and casually leaves civilization for the stark fields of the farming countryside. Finally, a tiny street sign, too small to honor the great Loyd Hall, can be seen if the driver is looking carefully. Missing the sign is much easier than finding

*Loyd Hall*

it, as most visitors have found. While Loyd Hall is a large and eye-catching edifice and is only a short distance down the road on the right, it still cannot be seen at this point due to the looming trees of old initially blocking one's view. This farm road, likely older than anyone can ever imagine, closely follows the once-wide Bayou Boeuf found on its left, now mostly naturally filled in by silt and debris from nature and human use for two centuries and more. This was Ralph Smith Smith's one-time river, once crowded with commercial boats carrying the local crops. It carried the crops also of William Loyd, the founder and builder of the stately Loyd Hall. Suddenly around a tree, a white sign pops up. We are finally here. This is Loyd Hall now seen through a grove of trees. The drive to this spirited dwelling was well worth it.

The origins of Loyd Hall are still not fully known. But the person who knows most about this grandiose dwelling these days, second, of course to the lingering ghost of William Loyd himself, is still here to tell Loyd Hall's tales of strife and elegance.

Ms. Beulah Davis, a youthful seventy-eight when I interviewed her, is both a genteel, handsome, and innately impressive woman. She was born outside of nearby Cheneyville, another jewel of history, about four miles from Lecompte. Her father was a sharecropper on the 450-acre Warner Grove Plantation. She has been living and working here at Loyd Hall for over half a century, since 1971 to be exact. She is as much a part of the history of Loyd Hall as the cypress walls of the edifice. She was originally hired as a housekeeper for the Fitzgerald family, one of over twenty different owners of this house over nearly two hundred years. The Fitzgerald family, headed by Dr. Frank Fitzgerald (1939-2020), an Alexandria veterinarian and his wife Anne, had three daughters to raise in this stately three-story mansion that they bought in 1948. One may ask why there are so many owners of Loyd Hall. Beulah explains, "Back in the day, there was no such thing as crop insurance. If your crops did well, you lived well. But if you didn't make enough on your crops any one year, you leased off your land or even sold your land. The house went with the land. And there were many a year that crops didn't do so well."

In 2006, one of the greatest preservationists of Louisiana in the twenty-first century, Michael "Mike" Jenkins of Alexandria, bought Loyd Hall. (Mike is also the owner of the monumental Hotel Bentley of Alexandria, which is discussed in this book.) Mike immediately began a restoration and updating process for Loyd Hall, a process which he still continues to this day. While Beulah may be the heart of Loyd Hall, Mike is the soul and protector.

I sat down with Beulah on Loyd Hall's back porch at a dining table on a very sunny, but still cold and wintry day. There was something truly relaxing in the feeling of sitting there just Beulah and I, as though nothing else mattered. Yet, I felt we were not alone, like sitting in the front of an airplane or bus and suddenly realizing all of the people who are behind you. But I felt that I was among friends from the past who wanted to hear what Beulah had to say today.

When asked if there were ghosts or spirits at Loyd Hall, Beulah had a lot to say:

> When I first came to Loyd Hall, I was very skeptical of any spirituality there. People told me about experiencing ghostly things while there. Sometimes people would say that you would hear footsteps and doors opening, but when they looked, no one was there.
>
> There would be times that you would smell the aroma of food, but there would be no cooked food exposed in the house. There would be times that you would see in your side vision something moving in the corner of the room. And sometimes when you would walk into rooms, you would feel a clammy cold feeling or a warm and steamy feeling. If it was a cold feeling, it was an evil spirit; if it were a warm feeling, it was a friendly spirit.
>
> Sometimes things would be moved from where I would put them. For example, when I set the table to eat, the silverware and napkins would be later moved to locations where I would never would place them. That was the spirits letting me know that they were here with me.
>
> What made a true believer out of me was that I could hear my name being called, 'Beulah.' And when I heard that, I was first thinking that I was imagining it all. I chopped it up to my imagination. But it would happen again, and again. The (Fitzgerald) family was living in the house then, so I thought they were home. But I checked upstairs and downstairs and found no one at home. No one but me was in the house. It wasn't until the third time that

all of this happened that I finally believed in spirits. The third time was the charm. If there were any spirits in the house then calling my name, it could only have been William Loyd himself. He was the builder and first owner of Loyd Hall. He was hung during the Civil War here.

During the Civil War, both Confederates and Union soldiers were stationed here at Loyd Hall. And Mr. Loyd wanted to be on the winning side of the war. In order to be on the winning side, Mr. Loyd had to play the Union army against the Confederate army. He was a "Double Spy." When the Union soldiers heard that he was trading their secrets with the Confederates, that he was a double agent going back and forth from one enemy camp to another, the Union soldiers arrested him and tarred and feathered him and hung him from an old tree on the front lawn. Mr. Loyd wanted to always be in control of everything he did, but his own family back in England disowned him because he was always causing trouble there. He was the black sheep of the Loyd family. His old family in England paid him the part of his inheritance that was coming to him and sent him from England to America, never to return. They made him change his name from having two "l"s to having one "l" in his name so he wouldn't be identified as being of the family of the famed Lloyds of London.

There is another ghost in the house along with William Loyd. During the Civil War, when the Union soldiers finally left, one of the soldiers deserted his regiment. He decided to remain at Loyd Hall because of his attraction to one of the young women of the house. The soldier, with the help of the young woman, hid out on the third floor of the house. When he was discovered hiding out by one of the family members, some say "Grandma Loyd," a fight occurred between them over the gun the soldier had kept. As they struggled over the gun, the gun went off and the soldier was killed. The soldier's name was Harry Henry and to this day, his blood stains are still on the third floor of the house. The family hid his body and buried it under the house in a shallow grave so the body wouldn't be found in case the Union soldiers ever came back to the house.

According to another former resident of Loyd Hall, every night at midnight, a man can be heard walking down the stairs to the second floor playing a violin.

I was taken up the steep steps up to the third floor by Beulah. The third floor is off limits to all visitors and was marked with a barrier crossing the steps going up from the second floor. Being granted special permission to go where few people these days would ever be allowed to go was both an honor as well as a treat. The third floor was large and tall in feeling due to the lack of furniture and decoration as well as the few walls that were up there. The floor was not lit and the only light, and shadows, were provided by the windows on the left and right sides of the floor. The entire floor was also very warm, almost humid, partly due to all of the heat in the house rising to that level, but possibly due to the good spirits that resided there, according to Beulah. Divided into three sections, with the center housing the rising staircase, Beulah showed me the right side of the house first. There, for the first time that I have ever seen, was what remained of a nineteenth-century school room. A dozen or so small old-time desks were bolted to linear boards that were attached to the floor, strangely all pointing angularly to the back right corner of the house. I could immediately see young children, real or imagined, sitting there, all proper and polite, learning from an unseen teacher. After looking in amazement for a few moments, now the desks were empty, covered with dust, waiting patiently for the children's return. The closed windows had old-time jail time bars covering them, possibly protecting people from falling to their death, or maybe keeping evil spirits out. Beulah did not reply when I asked her about the bars' purpose. But then we walked slowly over to the third section on the left side of the house. One would have to be blind not to see not one, but two unusually large blood stains on the floor, the one in the center larger than the other. Blood has a different consistency than any other fluid and when emanating from a human body, has a particular gravitational spray that no other fluid has. As I stared at the blood as though it were alive, Beulah said most assertively that samples of this stain have been tested, and the stains tested 100 percent as human blood. The rest of the floor was covered with a thin, fine layer of dust, but no dust seemingly covered the stains or surrounding floor. Yet, the blood was old, very old, having soaked deeply into the aged, somewhat now worn and splintered wood. I

*Harry Henry's blood, forever staining the floor of Loyd Hall*

leaned over and touched the stain, to the surprise and curiosity of Beulah. The stain felt gritty, yet my fingers slid over it like it still had a moment of freshness left. Beulah then ushered me out of there and down the stairs as though there was some urgency or fear. Again, no reasons were given by this soft-spoken and friendly woman. I felt sure that I saw the blood of Harry Henry, the Union soldier, and he wanted to continue his rest—possible only with our complete absence.

It is said that at a young age the Fitzgerald children have decided that they have seen a ghost. One day a Fitzgerald daughter asked her mother, "Did you see Harry today?" Ann Fitzgerald asked, "Who is he?" And the daughter replied, "Momma, that's our friendly ghost." From then on, the children reportedly delighted in terrorizing their friends with tales of Harry.

Down on the second floor, Beulah continued to tell me about the permanent residents of this house:

> There was another member of the Loyd family that died at Loyd Hall. She was Inez Loyd, a niece of William Loyd. She was engaged to be married, but her fiancé deserted her at the altar. She was very upset and distraught and soon threw herself out from the third-floor balcony and died.
>
> Sally Boston was a slave nanny that lived in the house with the Loyd family. She died very mysteriously. No one knows if she died of poisoning or was murdered some other way. There are times that you can get glimpses of a black woman dressed in white with a turban on her head and they assume it was Sally walking around. I feel that if the ghosts are really here, they are here to protect the house from the evil spirits.
>
> Some visitors want to come here to experience the ghostly apparitions, but it is actually the visitors who don't want to experience the paranormal who are usually the ones who actually do.
>
> Now some people who have stayed with us have woken up in the morning at five and smelled the aroma of food cooking. But no food was being cooked at that time. Way back when, they always began cooking food at that early hour.
>
> Some visitors have experienced someone sitting on their bed, yet no one was there. Or the lights would go on and off, or the shower floor was newly wet when there was no reason that it should be. Some visitors will see the rocking chairs on the porch suddenly start rocking even when there was no wind around. You can experience

> things here day or night; there's no particular time when the spirits become active.
>
> I tell everybody who comes here to have their own personal experience. The ghosts and spirits may scare you here, but they can't hurt you. Only the live ones can.

On sitting down again with Beulah at the back porch table, she carefully brought out a treasured collection of old, and some new, photos, one of which showed an elaborate wedding reception being held on the front lawn of Loyd Hall in 1978. This unnamed couple was dressed to the nines with handsomely dressed people pouring out of the front door of Loyd Hall onto the front lawn. After surveying the picture, Beulah pointed out a small curious image appearing to stand by the cannon, used by the house for decorative atmosphere, which was located on the front lawn also. Beulah said to me that the wedding couple came back later with this photograph and asked what the ghost was. Was it William Loyd, or the murdered soldier, or was it Sally Boston? Could it be another tragic death not recorded in the annals of Loyd Hall's history? This wasn't clear to Beulah or me as the spirit world doesn't always tell its story in an understandable way.

But what of the ghost of William Loyd himself? After some effort, I tracked down a very nice lady who was connected to Loyd Hall, now an executive secretary for Mike Jenkins, Ms. Felicia McCloud. Felicia has her own stories of the weird happenings at the house. She told me: "A visitor to Loyd Hall wanted to take a picture of the big house. There was a glare, so she moved over one step and saw an image of a man in old-fashioned clothes with a turn-down collar. One side of his face was normal, and the other side of his face was drooping, like a clown face. She looked away in surprise and when she looked back, the image was no longer there at the upstairs window. The window was in William Loyd's bedroom. The picture taker who saw the image said the man's deformed image was freaking her out."

This writer is by far not the first to question and to try to verify haunted happenings at Loyd Hall. In February of 2008, LSP Investigators came to visit. The group was represented by Jennifer Broussard of Lafayette and several others. The Central Louisiana chapter of the statewide group was headed then by Brandon Thomas and Brad Duplechien. The group set up shop at the historic home with the downstairs parlor becoming the command center.

According to the *Town Talk* newspaper, Thomas said, "In theory, ghosts are nothing but energy. Our bodies are nothing but energy and energy cannot be created or destroyed."

The *Town Talk* further said, "The goal of Louisiana Spirits is to scientifically explain phenomena that could be considered paranormal. For instance," Thomas said then, "a normal electromagnetic field reading should be between 0.5 and 1.0 Gauss. Gauss is a common unit of measurement of magnetic field strength. . . . In the field, you have to have an open mind and a closed mind at the same time."

The team used, among other devices: infrared cameras, digital voice recorders, EMF meters, and white noise generators for their searching.

As noted in the article and in other sources, Union Civil War soldier Harry Henry was one of the group's main focuses on that visit. Using luminol, the blood testing verification agent, the group tested the famous stain on the third floor. Once luminol was sprayed on the stain, the blood began to glow, a sure sign that it was blood, and a lot of it was present.

"After the luminol test, the team cut the lights and split into pairs," as noted in the *Town Talk* article, "(and) when the real ghost hunting began."

A week after the investigations, the recordings from the various devices were examined, and Jennifer Broussard noted "a couple of unidentifiable sounds" on the sound recordings. Investigator Lori Russell of Leesville reported, "There were a few strange photos and a few strange noises that we couldn't identify. I felt a brief cold spot in a room on the second floor. But that's just a little anomaly. It's hard to explain, but nothing to confirm." The group may not have found hard proof of spirits, but they did find blood, lots of it, and verified too.

Whatever the image, whatever the story, whoever the visitor, the permanent residents of Loyd Hall continue to walk the halls, look out of the windows, examine the decades of visitors that come to see and be amazed at the mysticism of Loyd Hall. When are you going to visit and have your own experience?

# Walnut Grove Plantation House

## "Who Is There? Friend or Foe?"

Walnut Grove plantation house is located about one-fifth of a mile southwest of Bayou Rapides and about two miles southeast of the town of Cheneyville. (Address: Route 1, Box 41, Cheneyville) The land is flat, and the bayou meanders around three sides of the home. At one time there was an extensive formal garden located in front of the ancient edifice. Although most of the plants are gone, five parallel brick paths were recently exposed in the front yard.

The house itself is an imposing two-story, five-bay, hip-roofed plantation style home with a modified central hallway plan and a hip roof. Originally, the lower hall was open to the outside. The upper hall has a side corridor which branches off at a right angle and terminates in a graceful fanlight-sidelight door combination at each end of the upper hall, which at one time were the main means of access to the formal room on the second floor. Back in the old days, there was a formal staircase and porch at the center of the house to give access to the hall. The only open galleries are at the rear. Most of the original paneled doors and windows are original as are the upper story floorboards. There was a considerable amount of reworking done to the ground floor in the early twentieth century in which a Queen Anne Revival–style stair and archway were installed and the old central hall was removed. The present front porch was added in 1927. The tin roof and rooftop hatch-way covering are apparently of recent construction. The house has the scars of cannonballs from Civil War era gunboats on Bayou Boeuf during the two invasions during the war.

One of the most unique features of Walnut Grove was the former small railroad which ran from the kitchen, located behind the house, to the dining

*Walnut Grove*

room, bringing hot foods to the family's table.

This plantation house was designed by Jabez Tanner (1810-1860) and was built in 1830. This two-story brick building is a fine example of Federal architecture and was added to the National Register of Historic Places on November 21, 1980.

There have been many reports over the years of spiritual happenings at Walnut Grove. Dr. Jill LeBlanc Larson who, along with her husband Paul, have owned Walnut Grove for the past twenty-seven years. Jill shared with me the house's following spiritual history:

> When we bought the place, the lady who we bought the house from did tell us that there were some rumors that the house was haunted. The original owners were Jabez and Esther Bettison Tanner (1815-1871). One of the kids, I think it was the older son, his name was Henry (1842-1927), had kids (himself) but they didn't live. They died when they were young. So he was known as Uncle Henry. And she always said that Uncle Henry either poisoned his wife's tea or his mistress's slave did. So that was the story and (Walnut Grove) is haunted by Uncle Henry. (Henry's wife was Mary E. Johnson Tanner, 1841-1899.)
>
> Well, not long after I've moved in here there were a few things that happened that I noticed, though nothing bad. For instance, I would leave the water on in the sink to defrost meat or something else, I would come back in and would find it (the water faucet) off. Or I would leave the lights on or off in the room and when I would come back in the room it was the opposite (of what it was positioned before). There were a few things like that happening. At first, I thought it was just me, but it continued to happen often.
>
> So the next thing that I noticed was in the mornings when I was getting ready to leave for work (as a dentist whose office is in Ville Platte), I would hear then somebody walking in the attic (of Walnut Grove). It was heavy footsteps. At first I thought it was squirrels or some animal. But it was a heavy person walking back and forth, back and forth. (For some strange reason) My husband could never hear it. It was obvious though, loud to me. I even went up there a

> couple of times to check and as soon as I got up to the top of the stairs, it would quit. So I kind of got used to hearing it.
>
> The other thing that happened was there was one area in a particular room, it only happened a couple of times. But when I walked into this room, there was like a cold spot in the middle of the room and it kind of smelled like perfume or flowers. That too kind of spooked me a little bit. Well I thought that this must be my imagination.
>
> But the thing that made me really believe (in ghosts) was that one day we were out working in the yard one day and this couple came driving by and visited with us. They were originally from here (in Cheneyville) but had moved to the north. They had come down back to visit with family. He was from here. He wanted to show his wife this place and he drove around it. When he was in college, he stayed here with the people who owned it then. . . . We started visiting with them and then invited them in. When we got to that particular room (where I smelled perfume and flowers) I had not said anything about what I had experienced in there. He (the visitor) told us that he used to experience a presence in this room. He said it was like a coolness and the smell of flowers. And that's when I first began to believe in ghosts living here.
>
> So the other thing is that my nephew saw a woman on the front porch a few times when he was working here in the summer. He described her as wearing an 1800s type dress. He was the only one who ever saw that. That just kept going on. And then when I was pregnant and had my first child, I never saw anything again. I thought it was odd not seeing and hearing of ghosts anymore. So one day I was talking to my mother about it, she said that she had gone in my house when I wasn't there. (She said) "I talked with the spirits and told them I was having some grandkids and I didn't want my grandkids to be scared and if they could please leave us alone." So I guess that had something to do with the spirits' departure. Ever since then, I haven't heard any walking in the attic. I never saw anything again. Nor have anybody else said about seeing anything. That's about it. I do believe these were spirits now, but didn't believe it when I first moved here. . . .

Maybe one day the ghosts will return to Walnut Grove. Maybe they will return when you have the opportunity to visit the lovely and historic Walnut Grove!

# Other Ghostly Spots in Rapides Parish

## "Everywhere You Go, They Are Waiting for You!"

There are sixteen ghost stories listed for **Alexandria** alone on the Ghosts of America website, including stories on the Diamond Grill restaurant, Bolton High School, the former Masonic Children's Home, Central LA State Hospital, and others. Here is just a sampling of two of the sites from the stories:

**Regarding the former Masonic Children's Home, Masonic Drive/LA Highway 165 South:**

"I am a resident of Alexandria, Louisiana, and once explored an old orphanage on Masonic Drive. I heard numerous rumors of the ghosts inhabiting the top floor of the main building (which has been abandoned for at least fifteen to twenty years), and everyone who has been there, including myself, has heard people laughing and having conversations and I heard someone saying, 'hello,' to me, but no one was there, and then I heard a loud thud and I ran away.

"I also occasionally see red eyes staring at me from a window when I pass. The eyes were too far apart to be a cat or animals and were very large. Also when I was exploring a boiler room in the complex, I saw floating orb-like things floating around. I definitely wouldn't recommend spending the night there, or even going alone."

**Regarding Bolton High School, 2101 Vance Avenue:**
"It was my freshman year at Bolton. I was walking with my friends to the homecoming dance. Before we walked in, we heard a loud thud. We looked around. We saw nothing. When we turned around, we saw a woman looking at us. We screamed then we ran away. Our math teacher came out of the auditorium. We told her what had happened. She said it was 'Gayle,' the ghost. She told us the legend about Gayle. At the end of the night, I saw the light on in the room where Gayle died in. I'm glad I don't go to Bolton anymore."

**Pineville** has one sighting on the Ghosts of America website:

**Regarding Central Louisiana State Hospital, Shamrock Street:**
"When I was little, my grandma worked at Central Hospital, and I would always stay late with her since she worked the graveyard shift. With her working at the switchboard, there were always things going on there.

"There was never a quiet night. I would always hear fainting, screaming, or footsteps and certain things like that. Being in the administrative building though, I always thought it was odd to hear those noises because all of the patients were in different areas of the property. But one night in particular it was a full moon, and the phone lines were going crazy because one of the patients kept saying that they saw Sally, a girl who escaped and jumped into the Red River not too far from the hospital.

"Knowing that it was a mental institution, though my grandma thought nothing of it, but I had a bad feeling about it. A few minutes later I heard whispering in my ear saying that Sally was here and when I turned around, no one was there. . . . Ever since then, I have believed in ghosts, and it seems that they want to attach themselves to me."

According to the Ghosts of America website, the following towns and communities in Rapides Parish have had at least one ghost sighting: Boyce, Cheneyville, Deville, Echo, Elmer, Flatwoods, Hineston, Lena, Otis, Sieper, and Woodworth.

According to the Ghosts of America website, the following towns and communities in Rapides Parish have had at least four ghost sightings: Lecompte.

According to the Ghosts of America website, the following towns and communities in Rapides Parish have had at least five ghost sightings: Forest Hill and Glenmora.

**Other Ghostly Rapides Parish Ghostly Locations:**

**An Unstated Location House in the Chambers community Near LSUA:**
"Reports range about this house from hearing strange noises and footsteps in the night to shutters that open by unseen hands." (*Cenla* Magazine)

**A Two-Story Unstated Location Frame House "Overgrown with Brush" in the Garden District in Alexandria:**
"Their ghost story tells of a woman who died in the house fourteen or fifteen years ago who still frequently visits her old residence. A light often appears on the second floor of the house, they say, although the building is believed to be unoccupied." (*Cenla* Magazine)

**The (former) Rapides Senior Citizens Home on Bolton Avenue in Alexandria:**
"According to several elderly visitors, the house was said to be haunted when they were children. Lucille Darby, former director of the center/home, said that assorted tales about the house and its owner, Susan E. Garner (1849-1940), led residents to believe that it was haunted. Legend says that Mrs. Garner, who died in 1940, had her casket built and her burial clothes laid out before she died. The coffin was apparently kept in a spare bedroom and, according to Mrs. Darby, Mrs. Garner often invited visitors upstairs to view her casket. This, along with the fact that she dressed in black and scolded children when they approached her yard, created a certain amount of mystique around the Bolton Avenue house and its owner." (*Cenla* Magazine)

Mrs. Garner lived a fascinating life. Here are excerpts from her *Town Talk* obituary:

"As soon as the death of Mrs. Garner was discovered, Mayor Lamkin phoned to relatives in Los Angeles, California, conveying the sad news of the death to her great-niece, Miss Mary Miles Minter, former famous movie star. Miss Minter and her mother, Mrs. Charlotte Shelby may come here, but will not be able to reach here before the funeral.

"Mrs. Sue Garner, aged ninety-one years, was the widow of the late Captain James N. Garner, who for many years operated the ferry boat on Red River between Alexandria and Pineville. Mrs. Garner had been a resident of Alexandria for three-quarters of a century. Her only son, Dr. N. B. Garner, who was a dentist by profession, died twenty years ago. She had lived alone in her Bolton Avenue home since the death of her son. . . .

"She passed away at her home sometime during Thursday night or Friday morning. Mrs. Daisy Converse, of the city clinic, was a friend of Mrs. Garner and frequently visited her during her last days. Mrs. Converse called at her home at noon yesterday and not gaining entrance she notified Mayor V. V. Lamkin, who instructed her to call for Officer Joe Baillio, a neighbor of Mrs. Garner, to go to the house and see about the reason for no answer being given to a knock at the door. Mr. and Mrs. Baillio and Mrs. Converse repaired to the Garner home at 4:15 p.m. and finding it impossible to gain entrance by the front door, found a window that could be opened, and when Officer Baillio entered the house, he found Mrs. Garner lying dead on her bed. . . .

"The Coroner notified District Judge R. C. Culpepper, who ordered all doors and windows sealed, and the keys are being held by the court until the arrival of near relatives. This action was taken for the reason that it was possible that Mrs. Garner was possessed of valuables that might be molested. Watchmen were placed at the house last night and today. . . ."

On Mrs. Susan Garner's tombstone at Old Rapides Cemetery in Pineville:

"Wife of James F. Garner/Mother of Nathaniel Branch Garner/Friends remove this slab and place me with my loved ones."

**A Large Two-Story House, Unstated Address, Near Rapides Regional Hospital in Downtown Alexandria:**

Had "unusual happenings" and received a "message from her house."

"'It started in my girls' room. She would stay until the night playing the piano.' One night while in bed, her daughter woke up screaming. She had seen a vision in the doorway. 'All the sounds and mysterious things started after that.'

"The residents first heard noises in the plumbing which sounded like water running through a pipe. The sound continued day and night for about a year, although plumbers were called out to check the pipes. 'We had a plumber come out here for four or five hours, but he never found anything,' she said. It wasn't too long after that they reported they reported hearing a humming sound in the wiring. 'I kept saying, 'Don't worry, we'll have it fixed,' but we had it worked on and once again, they never found anything.'

"The sounds soon moved into the walls, she said, creating a wave-like sensation. Her sister interpreted the sounds to be that of violins, while her daughter heard a sound similar to a dog whining. Whatever they heard, they knew it wasn't supposed to be there.

"This went on till 1978 when the sound began to ease. 'I believe that it was a message to me to get out. It was trying to scare me to death to get us out,' she said, explaining that as the years passed and the sounds continued, she was set on moving. 'The house was really too large for me. . . .'

"In 1976, the downtown residents decided to let the house go. She was hoping by not paying her monthly notes. . . . One afternoon, when she was $600 behind in her house payments, a man dressed in a black suit came to her door. 'He had a letter for me, but my dog was carrying on, so I asked him to drop the letter in my mailbox,' she said, adding that she was surprised at the puppy's actions. 'He usually didn't bark like that, and he was really acting up.' When she (later) reached into the mailbox, the box was empty. . . (she later found) that her back notes had been paid in full. . . ." (*Town Talk* Newspaper)

**The Remains of Camp Livingston, located on the service road east off LA Highway 167, near the intersection with the Shreveport Highway, north of Alexandria and Pineville:**

"Near the ice house at what remains of Camp Livingston, there is supposedly a group of lights which mysteriously appear above the trees and rise above the skyline. Some say that the lights are that of a lantern belonging to a headless man looking desperately for his head." (*Cenla* Magazine)

**The remains of Camp Claiborne, Intersection of LA Highway 165 and LA Highway 112, near Forest Hill:**

"At Camp Claiborne, tales have it that a man who was shell-shocked during World War II, dresses up in women's clothing and digs pits in which to capture unsuspecting victims." (*Cenla* Magazine)

**The Former Masonic Children's Home, Highway 165 South, Alexandria:**

"A grand home for its time, the children's Masonic Lodge served as a quality refuge for orphans for nearly seventy years. The home was initially built in 1925. The local Masons believed that the construction of this new home would advocate much better living conditions and an overall improvement in well-being, as opposed to the state-ran orphanages of the time, which were notorious for not being in the most optimum of conditions.

"The grounds initially consisted of a boys' dorm and a girls' dorm, with a chapel and large infirmary being built soon after. The lodge opened with its first residents, six young siblings, ranging from three to fifteen. The population soon grew quickly, as it is estimated that a total of 776 children once called this place home. The home finally closed in May of 1994, with the remaining ten children being moved elsewhere. The buildings have remained abandoned ever since.

"Roughly seven or eight years ago, plans to convert the grounds into luxury apartments were put into motion. For various reasons, contractors and repairmen began working in these buildings. It is here when reports of ghostly experiences began. We had interviewed several of these workers and most of them all had at least one interesting story to tell. Most common reports were seeing young children peering out the dorm windows at them, when the workers knew no one was inside. Additionally, these young guests enjoyed playing pranks on the workers as their tools would quickly disappear and show up in other locations.

Unfortunately, we were never able to obtain an investigation of the dorms, as we were extremely interested as to see what we may find there. Several years later, construction went into full force, as the two dorms were demolished to make way for the new apartments. However, the large three-story Italian Renaissance style infirmary still stands and will be used as the complex's office. . . ." (*Haunted Nation*)

**The Holloway (Methodist) Cemetery (also known as the Slay Cemetery), Slay Cemetery Road off Hickory Grove Road, Deville:**

"Located on the back roads of Deville, Louisiana, the Holloway Cemetery is one of the oldest, if not the oldest, cemetery in the surrounding area, having graves marked as old as the 1820s. The cemetery is quite large, yet the graves are spread out scarcely. The grounds are said to have contained a missionary and the site of several hangings from the massive oak trees present, yet no verifiable documentation has been found of these incidents. Sudden temperature changes and EMF spikes have been experienced here. . . .

"The cemetery was first brought to my attention by a good friend of mine that had also conducted a few amateur investigations here. On his most memorable visit, he and another investigator were walking around one of the large trees said to have been used for hangings. They were only equipped with an EMF meter, a voice recorder, and a flashlight; pretty much all we had back in the day. The two investigators began to feel an unexplainable cold spot. Keep in mind this took place in the middle of the summer and the words 'cold' and 'summer' do not go hand in hand in

Louisiana. They continuously ran their audio recorder during the strange experience. When they played back the audio, they heard a very chilling, no pun intended, voice saying, 'It's coldest right here!'" (*Haunted Nation)*

**Central Louisiana State Hospital Grounds, 242 West Shamrock Street, Pineville:**

"I don't know about you guys, but there is nothing more intriguing that an old abandoned insane asylum. With the amount of energy that is contained in this type of building, along with the sheer creep factor, a haunted asylum is at the top of any paranormal investigator's to-do list. . . .

"Over the decades, mental hospitals have grown to gigantic campuses of sorts, housing thousands of patients at any given time. One of the largest in America, actually still in operation, is the Central Louisiana State (Mental) Hospital in my current hometown of Pineville. The hospital was created by enabling legislation in 1902 to provide for the treatment of Blacks suffering from mental illness. The legislation was amended in 1904 to provide for the treatment of Caucasians as well as Blacks. The facility opened on January 6, 1906, and soon grew to epic proportions. During its peak operating year of 1959, the four hundred-plus acre hospital was home to over three thousand patients. At this time, and for years to come, the hospital would be the largest of its kind in Louisiana and one of the largest in the country. Today, Central Hospital has dwindled down to a mere shell of its former self, housing only a few dozen patients. . . .

"Up until today, the hospital has provided community-based living opportunities for those persons needing appropriate structure and support, care for short-term patients and specialized treatment for long-term individuals. Many of the original buildings on the large property have been demolished and replaced over the years. Similar to the Carville Leprosy Colony, over the years, the grounds would be a self-contained community within a community, housing several dorms, dining areas, tuberculosis ward, dairy barn, and machine shops. The oldest remaining buildings include (the) Rose Cottage (1917), the dairy barn (1923), the administration building and Fuqua Hospital (Unit 1) (1927) and Unit 3 (1937). The remaining buildings were constructed during renovations in 1942 or the early 1950s.

"The grounds are also home to a large cemetery that contains the burial sites of over three thousand patients that have died while they resided at Central State Hospital. Initially, the services were quite primitive, with the bodies being transported to the gravesite in a wheelbarrow until 1933 when a hand-drawn hearse was constructed. This hearse was used until 1950 and was pushed by pallbearers to the gravesite. Deceased female patients were draped in pink or blue shrouds made by the workers in the sewing room and the carpenter shop furnished coffins. A large wooden cross was placed to mark the cemetery on the hill in the early 1960s. A large white solid concrete cross has since replaced it. The cemetery was last used in June 1985.

"For years, whether it is due to urban legends or not, Central Louisiana Hospital has long been reported to being quite haunted by many of its former patients who died on the grounds. For obvious reasons, we (LSP) have been unable to investigate the dormitory areas of the hospitals (due to confidentiality), as patients have continuously lived here. We have, however, been able to investigate the oldest building on the grounds, the previously mentioned Rose Cottage. . . .

"Today, Rose Cottage is used as a small museum that documents the years of history for the hospital. Pictures are on display of some of the conditions from the hospital in its early years. Patients were literally placed in what looked like giant dog pens, individually isolated from one another, while others were tied up in large chairs and forced to sit there for hours without any stimulation or interaction. From 1941 to 1976, the building was also the site where electroshock therapy was administered. This is evident by the antique electroconvulsive machine that is still on display here. . . . One of the students (of a local high school) had advised me that her grandmother had long been a patient there and had regularly been exposed to the electroshock treatments which would eventually kill her as she died on the table during one of these sessions. . . ." (*Haunted Nation*)

The following is from Phillip Coco of Moreauville, Louisiana, a former addiction counselor at Central State Hospital:

"I have been in the (Central State Hospital) buildings late at night. You hear a lot of things in them, but you don't know what they are. You would hear a door closing on a different floor and you would go up there and there was nothing up there. Then you would hear a door closing on a lower floor and would go down and again there was nothing there. . . . Patients there have told me stories of their grandparents working there thirty or forty years ago. They said there were spirits on the third floor of the building we worked in which was the Fuqua Hospital building. There were all these noises up there (on the higher floors). I never determined whether I believed in the spirits or not, but there was definitely something there. I don't know for sure what it was.

"One of the things about Central is how many people are buried there. We really don't know (how many are buried there). There are thousands of people who are buried there. Many (of the graves) are not marked…There is a lot of history and question about some of the things that went on there. There was some pretty harsh treatment there back when mental health was not far advanced. Some pretty awful things happened there. . . .

"In the Fuqua building the stairwell was blocked off with heavy wire mesh like a cage. This was to keep people from falling or jumping down the staircase which went down to the first floor. . . . You had three to five thousand people living there at one time and they lived there their entire lives. . . .

"At the (old) dairy barn there were stories of questionable things going on that one just couldn't explain. . . . It had a haunted history also. . . . " (Personal Interview)

**Also on Central Louisiana State Hospital:**
"Unit two has an elevator that seems to be operated by unseen hands. . . . In the middle of the night, it will begin traveling between floors and opening and closing its doors with nobody on board. In other units, staff and patients have reported hearing doors slamming loudly and the sounds of heavy rolling objects echoing down the corridors. When the hallways are checked, they're empty and silent, and all the individual doors are firmly secured for the night.

"Unit seven stood unused for many years, but due to overcrowding and renovations going on elsewhere in the hospital, it was reoccupied in 1999. Shortly thereafter, staff and visitors began noticing an abundance of unexplained activity—strange glowing lights passing under doors, voices coming from empty rooms, unoccupied chairs suddenly tipping over, objects randomly falling from shelves, clocks keeping wildly inaccurate time, computers and electrical appliances turning on and off at odd times. . . ." (*Weird Louisiana*)

**Alexandria Zoological Park, 3016 Masonic Drive, Alexandria:**
"Featured on TV's *Ghost Hunters*, the zoo is said to be haunted by the spirit of deceased director Les Whitt, who passed away in 2008. He is said to play pranks and practical jokes from beyond the grave, just as he loved to do in life." (hauntedplaces.org)

**Formerly Sister's Restaurant (most recently known as Pitchers and Pints Brew House), 3231 Highway 28 East, Pineville:**
"One of the most popular hangout spots in the Pineville area is the Pitchers and Pints Brew House. The city is in short supply of watering holes since

the restrictions of being a "dry city" have been recently lifted. Still, the Brew House is a great place for a quick beer and a game of pool. Prior to the building being a bar, it was known as Sister's Restaurant and was owned by the parents of my co-founder and longtime friend, Brandon Thomas. Prior to being a successful restaurant, this place was host to many businesses such as a floral shop, veterinary clinic, insurance office, and a furniture store. The building was originally a private residence, built sometime in the 1960s. During this time, the original owner was conducting bulldozing work near the home when a freak accident caused a tree limb to fall off the dozer, decapitating him!

"Prior to knowing Brandon, I had frequented the restaurant as the food was quite good. Once I met Brandon in 2005, he would not only tell me that the restaurant belonged to his family, which would now enable me to get some great free food, but also that the restaurant had long been rumored as being haunted. As we were just starting out with Louisiana Spirits, we would often use the restaurant as our training grounds, along with many of the local cemeteries. I was always more fond of investigating here as it was climate-controlled, spider-free, and we had an endless supply of food at our disposal! In addition to all those perks, the restaurant did have its fair share of activity. On numerous occasions, we would be alone in the building and we could hear stacks of plates in the kitchen start to rattle as if they were moving on their own.

"The main resident haunting here is a young woman in a long black dress. For years, she has been seen wandering through the kitchen and dining area. Many who have seen her have described her as having long black hair, often appearing as if she is soaking wet. Cooks and waitresses have quit upon seeing her. In one memorable encounter, a new employee was using the restroom. As she sat in one of the bathroom stalls, she noticed the latch lift up and unlock on its own. The poor girl sprung from off the toilet and bolted out of the restroom with her pants still around her knees! She would never return to the restaurant again. Several guests had also reported seeing this woman walking by and mysteriously passing through the wall. On several occasions the alarm system had been activated, and when cleared, the alarm company stated that the system detected a "human figure." When police arrived, they would find no one in the building and no signs of attempted entry were detected.

"Once we had established Louisiana Spirits and acquired some legitimate investigators, we would return to the restaurant to investigate. We would turn to the help of our friends, a husband and wife duo, who were both legitimate sensitives and could accurately detect the presence of a spirit in a given location. . . . Without giving them any history of the location or of the descriptions of the entity, we brought our friends to the restaurant to see what they could detect. They quickly picked up on a strong female presence radiating from the seating area, back to the dry food storage area. A slight detection of a young girl was also felt, but it was determined she wasn't a permanent fixture. When our friend was asked to give a description of the woman, she was observed wearing a long dark dress and appeared to be soaking wet! I would say that is a pretty accurate description by any accounts!

"Further research of the property taught us that to the rear of the restaurant, only a couple hundred feet, was a small body of water known as Bayou Maria. The water is merely a stream by today's accounts but during the nineteenth century, Bayou Maria was one of the major channels of water in the area, allowing merchants and travelers alike to easily maneuver through the city, through the Bayou Maria Basin, ultimately emerging into the mighty Red River, which could take individuals anywhere in the state. Consider Bayou Maria as a back alley way if comparing to a major street system. It is unknowing as to what sorts of dastardly acts may or may not have taken place along these backwaters, but the odds are definitely there.

"Without telling our sensitive friends about this discovery, we would return for a nighttime visit of the restaurant and we would once again, bring them along. Early into the investigation, we entered the dry food storage area, which was where our friends first sighted the woman in black. We noticed a drop in temperature, followed by a brief EMF spike. At this time, one of our sensitives was able to obtain a visual of the young woman. The eye contact was very brief, but she was able to get a little more detail. From her recollection, the young woman's name was Charlotte and she had drowned in nearby waters. Like I said, our friends knew nothing of the history, nor did they know about the now near-extinct body of water to the rear of the building. I have always had my doubts about people who claim they are sensitive, as there are many charlatans out there. However, such as with this case, when people are able to give you such a detailed report of something that you know they knew nothing about, you cannot help but be fascinated. Charlotte then quickly retreated, not being encountered the rest of the night. Throughout the remainder of the investigation, things would stay quite calm.

"Today, as the music blares and patrons enjoy a few beers over a game of pool or darts, they are either too busy or too inebriated to notice any strange events at the bar. However, this does not mean that the hauntings have subsided. On several occasions, we have spoken with the new owners of the building, and they have indeed confirmed that they, as well as fellow coworkers, have had unexplainable experiences during late hours when customers have left for the night. When asked where the ghostly encounters were mostly experienced, they all said the back portion of the kitchen area, which was the dry food storage area during the times as a restaurant. When also asked, "What did you see?" we were not surprised to hear the description of a woman with long black hair wearing a long black dress. After we asked if the woman appeared to be wet, the manager promptly asked, 'How did you know!?'

"In my opinion, I feel that the resident haunting, Charlotte, is simply a residual energy of a tragic event that took place here years ago. Either accidental or intentional, her death involved water in some way or another, whether she drowned or her body was disposed of here. The fact that she seemed to be contained primarily in the area where the dried food storage area was in is not an uncommon event, especially with a residual haunting. With this type of energy, they are unaware of their surroundings. This portion of the building was added on in later years and it is uncertain as to what stood here prior to the remodeling. Another good example of this is when a spirit is witnessed walking through a home's wall or they are only seen from the waist on up, as if they are walking ground level on a raised home. Further research would show that the home either had walls or additional rooms added or the spirit is attached to a previous home that was built on the ground. The residual energy is obviously unaware of the renovations, as they are simply etchings in time. They aimlessly roam around, reliving their past lives, not acknowledging any refurbishments such as new walls or elevated floors." (*Haunted Nation*)

# Ghostly Investigator Teams

# Mimi's Ghostbusters

## "Who Are You Going to Call?"

We've all seen on television and read about some "ghost busting" type teams who roam around old abandoned and often dilapidated places like asylums and hospitals across America. Both the teams and ourselves are fascinated with the journey of exploring these types of facilities. Even those people who don't really believe there are ghosts want the teams to find something, anything, that might be considered "ghost-like" or ghost connected.

I'm not sure if any of these teams anywhere can be defined as "professional." Their exploits purport as scientific, but the science establishment in general does not recognize "ghostbusting"-type investigators. Yet, what many of the teams use to varying degrees is scientific-type equipment, equipment that logically could intercept and identify the movement and radiating power of the spirit world. Everyone has their own opinions on this, but obviously the majority of people are interested in what these teams do as these teams have successful television programs that often run for years.

One of Louisiana's most popular and intriguing teams is "Mimi's Ghostbusters." "Mimi," better known in the non-spirit world as Brenda Frick of Lafayette, Louisiana, describes her group as follows:

"My name is Brenda Frick, better known as '*Mimi*'! I am the organizer of '*Mimi's Ghostbusters!*' We are *not professionals!* You only need six things to join our group!

1—Camera or iPhone
2—Flashlight
3—Rubber Boots
4—Mosquito Spray
5—Ghost Buster's T-Shirt
6—Depends (In case you get the piss scared out of you!)"

Mimi went on to tell me about her team's experience at Loyd Hall:

> Loyd Hall Happenings:
>
> Number one, Slave Cemetery: We all jumped in the back of a pickup truck, not the driver (of course), in search for the slave cemetery! We did this during the day and in the middle of the night! The nighttime is way more scarier of course.
>
> Number two: We each took turns locked in a room alone for four minutes! You have no light or phone while in there! One of my ghostbusters went in there for her turn and came out hysterically screaming with chest pains! We gave her nitroglycerin and rushed her to the (nearby) Bunkie hospital! After a full evaluation, not once but twice, (they) found absolutely nothing wrong with her. . . .We believe this maybe was a ghost encounter?"

Mimi provided me with a list, in no particular order, of her complete ghostbuster team:

1—Charlotte Murray
2—Gwen Ruppert
3—Fane Ruppert
4—Brandt Ruppert
5—Madylin Fritsche
6—Tracy Bryant
7—Margaret Bryant
8—Melissa Ritchie
9—Sarah Richardson
10—Lora Frick
11—Colin Frick
12—Susan Hines
13—Mackenzie Ritchie
14—Mollie Goldman

15—Beverly Ducote
16—Michelle Murray
17—Debi Kinsey
18—Sue Gomez
19—Jodene Word
20—Mary Helen Lett
21—Jennifer Williams
22—Stephanie Bailey
23—Kathy Daniel
24—Lauren Stelly
25—Skye Greene
26—Hadley Greene
27—McGuire Ellis
28—Cathy Courville
29—Courtney Weimann
30—Lexie Harbstreit
31—Zack Cook
32—Lauren Pogue

*Mimi and some members of her ghostbusting team*

Mimi adds: "I would never go ghost hunting if I did not have my backup! My backup being *Mimi's Ghostbusters!* That is a fact!"

I met with a portion of the team at the lovely and historic (and haunted) Loyd Hall one spring morning. The members of the team present that day had just spent the night there, a visit that they often repeat there. We all sat around a long and ancient dining room table that was mostly surrounded by floor to ceiling windows looking out on the backyard of Loyd Hall. Sitting there, one cannot help but feel like the many owner families that must have also sat there looking out on the fields of cotton that once proliferated the area. The members of the team that I sat with that day were all regular, common-sense people coming from different perspectives, all believing in one thing—that the spirit world is alive and among us on earth. And the members of the team were going to find evidence of the spirit world while having fun and comradery too!

The group had so much to say! Brenda has been a shoe salesperson at Dillard's Department Store in Lafayette for seventeen years. Here's Brenda/"Mimi" starting off the conversation:

> I started doing this seven years ago because for the last twenty-five or thirty years, I have been doing (visiting) fake haunted houses with my daughter and others. And heck, it was getting expensive, what have you. Well, you go that often, you get used to where the people in costume hide and come out and say "Boo" and try to scare you. I was finally done with that. You do that long enough and you can figure out where they are hiding so I decided why even go anymore. So one day I was watching the ghost (SyFy) channel and said, "Oh, I think I want to try and go to a real haunted house." So seven years ago, I looked up about haunted houses and found The Myrtles in St. Francisville (LA). That was the first place I went to. I have been going there for seven years now. So that's how it all started. . . . When I made the decision to do this, I initially had four ghost busters, including me. The rest of the people that I know thought I was nuts. (They said) "You're stupid, you're this and that." I said to them, "To each his own." Today, I have a team of thirty. We don't all do (on visits to haunted places) at the same time because everyone has issues, you go to work, you don't have a sitter, for whatever reason. The most I've had at one time together is twelve to actually go to a haunted house to spend the night. I actually like to rent the whole place (the haunted house) so strangers are not there telling you stuff like, "We can't sleep, you need to quiet down, or we are going to call the manager. I solve that distraction by wherever we stay, we rent the whole damn place. . . ."
>
> Loyd Hall: I've probably been here four times including this trip. . . . We've found lots of "orbs," a few ghost faces, and what have you. I've never seen anything anywhere I've been with just your naked eye. But when you go home, you check out what you have recorded on your phone and it's like "Oh my God," you see stuff. You study what you see, and it jumps out at you. So I don't know, but we go from room to room and have all the lights turned out. We just have one little candle with a cross on it in there and we try to get the ghosts to come out. (In advance) We try to learn the history of who might still be inhabiting here, who hasn't crossed over yet.

Let's start with (William) Loyd (the builder of Loyd Hall). We learn his history, how he lived, how he died, the whole ball of wax. We are trying to do that throughout the night. We go from room to room. We are not just seeking Loyd, but looking for evidence of Harry Henry, the military man who got killed, as well as the little slave girl who would go around and was terrified of the fire, so before she would leave her room, she would blow the candle out. (We are interested) In that kind of stuff. And we continuously stay up and do it until we can't stay up anymore. We try to find proof of the ghost world. I already knew that when I first went ghost hunting that ghosts were real. . . . I don't understand it and I think that's what keeps drawing me back. And probably if something ever happens to me, because some of my ghost busters have gotten hurt, though not at Loyd Hall, (if something happens to me) I'm done. (She laughs loudly)

I don't know. I love the history. I love the architecture, the furnishings . . . just all of it combined. But I would not do this by myself ever because I am the (most easily scared) one out of the bunch (the team). . . . When I've got to have a buddy (fellow team member) go with me to the bathroom, that's being scared. They all know that (laughs), okay?

Here (Loyd Hall) was my biggest experience. Ahhhhh. . . . Nothing happened here as far as getting clawed or taking a demon home with you, that's happened elsewhere, just not here. It's ghost pictures (I've seen), a lot of, lot of orbs. . . . I've put the candles out on the fireplace mantel, turned out all of the lights and sat in the dark. You have to have a camera or iPhone. When we're here, we jump from room to room. If nothing is happening in one room, we jump to another room all night long. When you go back into the room and it's like, every single time, my candles, they're not real, I don't want to burn the plantation down, they're LED, they were on, lit when we walked out, when we went back in (the same room), they were off and the switch was now in the off position. And I told Miss Beulah (Davis, seventy-eight-year-old, longtime manager of Lloyd Hall), and she said, "Yeah, yeah, that's Sally, the little slave girl. She's scared that you're going to burn the plantation home down. . . ." I do have an alarm (device) that I put out that if we are mainly like we are not on the first floor, (I put it) on the piano. It's off right

> now because people keep passing in front of it. But if we are on the second floor or the attic (third floor), and we hear the alarm (it's motion censored), we run down to see if we catch that ghost on camera or your eyes and it's like we don't see anything.
>
> We've smelled bacon here before in the middle of the night. I'm not talking about when they cook it for breakfast here. We're coming down the stairs and smell (she reenacts here the act of smelling) and wonder, "What's behind me?" The smell comes out of the middle of nowhere. . . . The ghost pictures I have showing faces in a window, in mirrors, etc. It's almost like a portal to hell, to be honest. You see faces, like they are looking at you.
>
> So I just don't know (what my biggest spiritual experience is). It's just all of it that keeps calling me back. I love it. I love it!

When I asked Mimi what got her first interested in anything spooky or haunted in nature, she said this:

> My daughter from Houston, Texas, came home once in October. She said, "Mom, if I wanted to go to a fake haunted house, would you go with me?" I said Yeah. But my daughter said, "I mean for you to get out of the truck and actually go inside with me, not just stay and sit in the truck." And I went. Where the hell would I go? And that was it after that. The whole month of October doing Halloween stuff—dressing up for Halloween costume contests. The most we won was three grand. We went to fake haunted houses every weekend. We would go to cemeteries. It just kept rolling. But that's how it all started way back thirty years ago. . . .
>
> I was born October 31, 1951, on Halloween. And I tell people, "Yes, I am a witch." I'm not really, but you know what I am saying. (laughs)

**WRITER'S NOTE:** The group defined "orbs" as circles of light where there shouldn't be any. Two of the ghostbusters showed me pictures showing these orbs. They looked like circles of translucent color that cannot be explained by me. Most unusual!

Along with Mimi this date were six other members of Mimi's Ghostbusters. Margaret Bryant of Marksville is a cafeteria worker at Lafargue School. She spoke next:

> My experience with haunted houses is just that we like to go and see if we can see anything. I've never seen anything with the naked eye, but like what Mimi said, we see stuff on our phones like orbs and hear noises sometimes, things like that. It's very exciting to hear and see these things and to be present in a haunted house.
>
> At Loyd Hall, we have experienced lots of orbs (seeing them) on our cell phones. . . . I have come here (Loyd Hall) twice, and the orbs are most of what I have seen. . . . I like being with these ghostbusters. It's an experience that we all share. (laughs)

Tracy Bryant of Marksville, Margaret's first cousin, describes her employment as "I sell cigarettes to the incarcerated." She then spoke: "Orbs are like balls of light. And some people say that they (the orbs) cannot be discounted as dust. I feel they are spirits that travel as little orbs of light that are trying to manifest. . . ."

Tracy then showed me a picture from her iPhone of her adult son standing next to an old wooden door in the attic of Loyd Hall. She continued:

> He had just opened up the crawl space of the attic. The legend is that Harry Henry (the Union soldier during the Civil War who was hiding out at Loyd Hall) was in the attic hiding. (The orb is the spirit of Harry Henry still living in the attic.) In addition to the orb in this picture, there is a misty area and my son's hand is not in focus. . . . (Tracy showed me the various spiritual aspects of the family.) I know it is hard to see here because there is a lot of light on this picture, but when you take it and look at it in a darker area, it comes into vision. . . .
>
> I joined Mimi's Ghostbusters seven years ago. Back then, my (then) thirteen-year-old daughter was interested in going to another plantation home. We called Aunt Brenda (Mimi) as she was big into ghost hunting and ghosts. So maybe she could help us find a ghost or experience a ghost. So that's how I got involved in the ghost busting club. She (Mimi) said she was coming here (Loyd Hall) and said it was only thirty minutes (drive) and said, "Why don't you come?" So we came to Loyd Hall.
>
> I actually didn't experience any ghost sightings here, but we did get pictures of orbs and such. We heard creeks and crevasses in the attic and on the stairs and the candles (suddenly) going off (by themselves). It's just the mystery of whether we will hear something or see something (that makes it special for me). So I like it a lot.

> I do believe in ghosts. I believe that I have a ghost in my own home from a man who used to live on the property. The reason I say that is that I was trying to sell my property. I was really close to him (the ghost). He was my employer. I was really close to him. I bought the land (and house) when he died. And I was going to sell my home. It was really big and (I wanted to) downsize. He opened and closed the doors and broke a wine glass out of our shelf where we hold wine glasses. He slung a wine glass down and broke it on the floor. I definitely believe in them and (blame them) for not being able to sell my home. . . .

The next ghost buster to speak was Gwen Ruppert, wife of Fane Ruppert and a niece of Mimi. She is the CEO of the YMCA in Corpus Christi, Texas. She said:

> First and foremost, the reason why I come is truly for my aunt Brenda. She gets all of us together and it's for the live people. We really enjoy one another's company, and we get to giggle and experience one another while we are looking for the dead. You know it's just the excitement of trying to capture somebody or something. My aunt Brenda, she is just really so excited, and we're excited for her and it's just a lot of fun. We laugh a lot, but there is some seriousness to it too because we realize that a lot of this is real. We do walk among spirits and possibly demons. It's all in the Bible. All throughout the Bible, Jesus is casting out demons, so here at Loyd Hall when we go up into the different areas on the plantation, as my aunt Brenda referred to, you like to know the history of the place you are exploring. When you are talking, you are asking for Mr. (William) Loyd, you are giving him credit for the beautiful plantation. You're asking Mr. Loyd to make himself present. And the one thing that I saw, your heart begins to race a little bit. All of the lights are out and it is so dark and you are actually trying to taunt the spirits to manifest themselves. And you're just trying to be quiet and any little noise (is noted). You're taking pictures. And when you actually go back to look at your pictures, you see a mist and look at it. A face appears. And that's when you are like, okay, could that be Mr. Loyd. . . .
>
> Do we know (for sure)? We'll never know. It's just the whole experience of it all really makes it really cool. I have to give credit to Miss Beulah and her history here on the plantation. . . . This house

> has just stood here, and imagine everything that has passed through it in time. So we are just here in this moment in time. I think about everything that has come before us and the remnants that will still be here from that time. . . .

Gwen's husband, Fane Ruppert, who works at a manufacturing plant, shared the following:

> I don't really have a lot to share other than I would say that last night was probably somebody (Fane) in training. . . . It was very interesting to see all that, how they all did it, the drawing out stuff. The drawing out sometimes was to egg them on a little bit if they (the spirit world) weren't listening. (laughs) It started out trying to do the normal stuff, call them out, you hear, "Do you want us to leave?" Things like that. We kind of hang out in rooms and then move on. Some rooms are supposedly worse than others. It's all very interesting. I wish that I would have seen more. But the hardest thing is just trying to figure out how to stay up that long. (big laugh) Especially after what you had, an Easter weekend. But for now, I would like to do it again. This group (that stayed last night) was (primarily) a girl's group, a women's group. I mean that for the most part. It's like your bunko club and you have subs. So I jump in as a sub. But other than that, I would like to do it again. This was my first night here or in any (haunted) house. . . .

The next member of Mimi's Ghostbusters is Brandt Ruppert, the son of Fane and Gwen Ruppert. He is a caretaker for persons with intellectual disabilities. He said:

> My name is Brandt. This is my first night at ghost busters and first night at Loyd Hall. I kind of have a different experience than everybody else had. I didn't see anything last night, and I didn't photograph anything on my phone as well. But just pulling into the Loyd Hall property, I was just taken back by the view of the property and the historical aspect of the property and how it's maintained and kept. You can kind of get that feeling that you are stepping back in time when you come here.
>
> I really truly feel that the spirits that are in Loyd Hall are more of a protective spirit. . . . I've read the story that the house stood vacant

> for seventeen or eighteen years and wasn't vandalized during that time. And I believe that that occurred for the reason of the spirits inhabiting here that are protecting this house. . . . I was never really spooked when I stepped in the house, but I felt that someone was with us. They are not necessarily a bad thing or a scary thing, but it was a good thing. . . . While we were moving through the house, you just feel that there is someone there with you. . . . It was just comforting being here. So that is my experience being at Loyd Hall.

The last speaker was Madylin Fritsche, the fiancée of Brandt Ruppert. Both are from Kearney, Nebraska. She said:

> My name is Madylin. Brandt really took the words out of my mouth. He said everything that I was going to say. I love me some good architecture, so when I walked in here, it was really cool. I've never stayed in any place this big and historical before. I really like that aspect and seeing Aunt Brenda (Mimi) doing her thing. It was really sweet to see how passionate she was about it. This is my first time being here at Loyd Hall and being part of this. I am really thankful that I get to be a part of this. . . . I really like the vibe of all of this. Aunt Brenda asked, "Are you sure you want to do all of this?" Exactly what Brandt said, I felt safe here and didn't feel like I was in danger really. . . . They (the spirit world) wants to co-exist here with you. I had a good time.

When I asked for the "biggest" spiritual experience that any of the group had, Mimi had this wonderful story:

> Well, it's The Myrtles (Plantation Home in St. Francisville) all day long. I've probably gone there ten times over the last seven years. One of my ghost busters had been clawed, her whole back, by three finger nails, clawedddd (she made a loud scratching sound). Her whole back is burned. It's red. They're screaming, "My back is on fire, fire." She had three layers of clothes on and a shirt. On the property (there at The Myrtles) in the gazebo is where it happened. We all ran back to the plantation home, ran upstairs, and took everything off. It was like, "Oh my God!" Her whole back was burned. She kept saying it was on fire. We checked her three layers of clothing out to see what had happened (and found nothing in

the clothing). For that to happen, her shirt would have had to be ripped or get a snag or whatever. There was nothing. Her clothes were perfect. Her shirts were perfect, all three of them. Everything was perfect. It was like, "Wow." So we went back to the gazebo to see if she had bumped into thorns or whatever to try to be able to say it wasn't a demon. There was nothing there to cause that. It was impossible for anything earthly to cause that. That was Mackenzie, one of my ghostbusters. She wasn't scared of anything until then. She was probably my bravest ghostbuster, the bravest one out of the whole bunch. We were all scared at that point. She went back on the property and said she was going to walk the property again. "You are going to walk the property again?" I asked her, "With what you got on your back?" "It's okay, I'm not scared," she said to me. And she did. That's one trip.

Then my grandson came. It was his first time at The Myrtles. . . . He said to me that he wanted to go on one of these excursions. He was fixing to be thirteen. So for his thirtieth birthday, unlucky thirteen, I decided to take him to The Myrtles and pay for him and his best friend and give them a room. We would have the whole plantation. We would have no strangers present. And his mom came with us also because she wasn't too sure about all of this. She had never gone on one of these ghostbuster trips before.

When we started that night, I picked the "soldier room" to check out first. The four of us got into the bed. We had our tape recorder running. He (the soldier) lost a leg during the Civil War. Like Loyd Hall, they made these homes during the war like field hospitals. . . . We were in the bed Indian style. My grandson was at the head of the bed, and I was in front of my grandson and so forth. So when I sat down Indian style, my rear end was actually sitting on the toes of his shoes. He had some tennis shoes on. I could touch him. I knew he was back there. So we started to try to contact the soldier. We asked him, "Do you want us here?" We ask all these questions; I don't remember the particular questions. The lights were out. All I had was this little bitty cross (LED) candle. I asked Colin (the grandson) if he was okay before we turned the lights off and he shook his head (yes) and didn't speak. The next thing you know, he is screaming to the top of his lungs! I can't say this now whispering, "Mimi, Mimi get it off!!" (Mimi is yelling all of this) "Get it off me Mimi, get it off! It's burning, it's burning, it's burning!!" And he jumped out of the bed to go to the door. It's dark now and I'm screaming for. . . I do use foul language, so can you edit my (testimony)? Do you want to hear the way it really came down? (I responded yes.)

He's screaming and is at the door by then. The lights are out and I'm screaming for Mackenzie to turn the f——g lights back on. Turn the f——g lights on! Turn the f——g lights on! He's screaming and he's standing there and he's literally is white like that sheet of paper right there (points to a blank sheet of paper). And I said, "Oh my God Colin." He said, "Mimi, take it off me. It weighs like a hundred and forty pounds! It's heavy, it's heavy." I said we've got to carry him out of here into the seating area at The Myrtles. He continues to scream, "My leg, my foot, my leg, it's on fire, it's on fire." When I pulled his pants leg up and he's still screaming to get it off him, I said, "Colin, Colin, Mimi doesn't see anything, doesn't see anything. So I can't get it off you!" I literally couldn't see a damn thing. I pulled his pants leg completely up and he had these three claw marks from the middle of his foot, his instep, the top of your foot, it had gone up his leg, not too far up his leg, probably about six inches. The (claw mark) started in the middle. He kept on saying that it was on fire, it's hot. The red made a circle there. Finally, I told Mackenzie to go get his (Colin's) mother. She was too scared and was outside sitting in the courtyard. To make a long story short, she came in and said, "Okay Mimi, I know you are acting." We were all crying upstairs. She said, "Ya'll are doing pretty good (acting)." I told her, "This s—t is real, this s—t is real. Lord, you're going to kill me." When she saw his leg, she said, "We're getting f——g out of here! Get packin'!" My (fellow) ghost buster said to me, "What are we going to do?" And I said, "Just do whatever she says." She yelled again, "Just throw everything in a bag; we're getting out of here." So just before midnight, we went to another hotel and made sure my grandson was okay. The weight had lifted off him, but it was still burning. We waited till morning to go home.

To round all of this off, my grandson did have to go see a priest. . . . The priest said in front of his (Colin) mom and dad, "And who were you with?"

I almost lost my son over all of this. He almost disowned me. . . . My daughter-in-law said, "Who loves him more than Mimi/ Who knew that was going to happen?" For a year after that, ghost hunting was not even mentioned. Me and my son did not talk very

> much that year. We're okay now, but he didn't talk to me very much that year.
>
> When my grandson turned fourteen, he told me, "I'm ready to go back." What happened with these claw marks and burns, they lasted about three days and then just vanished…

Gwen Ruppert then shared this story:

> I went to the Ott Hotel in Liberty, Texas, as a Mimi's Ghostbuster. And I do caution anybody that is thinking about going in and looking and searching for the spiritual realm because I do think there is a fine line between spirits and possibly demons because at the Ott Hotel we had fun, and it's all fun and games to be there and scared and the frivolous nature of things. But sometimes things can get scary in that realm on a whole different level. I really feel that I was affected a little bit because after leaving the Ott Hotel, I heard about these attachments. I am a Christian and about the time I went to the Ott Hotel I had not been to church for a year and I had been experiencing seizures at night. I was falling out of bed. I was having nightmares and would wake up and go to the bathroom. And in the bathroom (I was so sick) that I would fall into the wall. Strange things would be happening to me. And then I really started going back to church and all of that (bad) stuff stopped. So I do caution people to keep it on the lighter side of things because it (the spiritual world) is real. You have to be careful with what you are dabbling in, so to speak. . . .

Mimi's Ghostbusters is an impressive group. I kind of hope they will ask me to join one day!

The spirit world in Central Louisiana reacts to different people in different ways. How will they react to you?

# Louisiana Spirits Paranormal Investigators

## "They Do What They Do for All of Us!"

Ghost hunting shows are popular and fascinating among the many enthusiasts of those shows. People are simply fascinated with not only the spirit world but also with those who hunt for the spirit world. The interest in ghost hunters clearly goes back hundreds of years, back to the innate want to solve crimes and the creation of the crime/murder detective. We just don't want to see the spirit world exposed; we want to be part of the satisfaction of exposing the world ourselves. It is the proverbial "thrill of the chase." Ghost hunting and ghost hunters have tapped into this thrill, this want of being a part of the case. The journey to the destination in this case is often better than the arrival to the scene.

The LSP investigative group is very similar to the nationally known TAPS group, but by definition, the LSP group is an exclusive statewide group that almost entirely visits only Louisiana locations. (According to the LSP website, on rare occasion they did prepare reports on a few out of state places including two places in San Diego, California, including the historic Hotel Del Coronado.)

According to their website, they introduce themselves in the following manner:

> Hello and welcome to the website of LSP Investigations! We are a serious group of professional and analytical individuals, dedicated to the investigating and research of paranormal activity. If you, or someone you know, are dealing with paranormal activity in your

> home or business, please contact us! All of our services are free of charge and remain confidential unless you give consent to publish our findings.
>
> Hello, we are Brad Duplechien and Brandon Thomas, Founders of LA Spirits. We strive to be the premiere paranormal investigative group in Louisiana. We created this group not only to seek answers for ourselves, but to educate and assist others in a field that is respected by few, yet intriguing to all. If you have any questions or need any help, please contact us.
>
> We are proud to be the only paranormal investigative group in the state that regularly covers every inch of Louisiana! By being divided into six fully functional and self-contained chapters, we can easily dispatch a team to any location in the state.
>
> Boasting one of the largest caseloads of any group in the country, we are proud to be Louisiana's oldest and most structured investigative team with a reputation that is second to none! We provide confidential and professional services to our clients consisting of quality investigations, detailed reports, and courteous follow-ups, putting our referral system in a league of its own.

According to their current website, the members of the Central Louisiana team include:

Grady Welch as case manager
Bree Hegwer as co-case manager and lead investigator
Amber Wisinger as investigator
Len Binning as investigator

In an interview with the Alexandria *Town Talk* newspaper, founder Brandon Thomas said, "In theory, ghosts are nothing but energy. Our bodies are nothing but energy and energy cannot be created or destroyed. . . . The goal of Louisiana Spirits is to scientifically explain phenomena that could be considered paranormal. For instance, a normal electromagnetic field reading should be between 0.5 and 1.0 Gauss. (Gauss is a common unit of measurement of magnetic field strength.) In the field, you have to have an open mind and a closed mind at the same time." The team used, among other devices: infrared cameras, digital voice recorders, electromagnetic field meters, and white noise generators in their searches. You may not always agree with whether ghosts and the spirit world exist, but these good and knowledgeable people do their best to bring out the truth for all to see and understand.

LSP has visited many sites in Central Louisiana, especially in Rapides Parish and Alexandria. Here is a summation of some of the reports from the LSP publicly accessible website:

## HISTORICAL LOCATIONS

**The Rose Cottage Museum, Central Louisiana State Hospital Grounds, 242 West, Shamrock Avenue, Pineville:**

The Rose Cottage is a small, two-story, concrete, Renaissance Revival–style structure located in a park-like setting on the grounds of Central Louisiana State Hospital (CLSH) in Pineville. This 1917 building retains its architectural integrity because it has been little altered over the years. Built originally as a pathology laboratory, this simple, but imposing structure features two major rooms and a stairway all on the ground story with a single long room on the upper story. The Rose Cottage is locally significant in the area of architecture as a landmark within the context of the City of Pineville which has retained relatively few fifty plus year old buildings.

The architect for Rose Cottage was Joseph Hermance Carlin (1869-1923), chief carpenter, from Rayne, Louisiana. He was a patient of CLSH from September 13, 1909, to August 1, 1912. He served as both the architect for Rose Cottage and as the "builder" of the famed hospital's dairy barn in 1923 shortly before his death.

The Rose Cottage housed the CLSH's laboratory and morgue. As such, it was the hub of the institution's diagnostic procedures, as well as serving as a center of learning and teaching. A 1922 report by H. L. Johnson, MD, pathologist, listed fifty-six postmortems conducted there. In 1928, 27 autopsies were reported by Robert H. Foster, MD and in the two-year period from 1932-34, when 8,308 laboratory procedures were done, Foster reported sixty-three "necropsies" out of 186 deaths. Dr. Arthur Seale (1904-1999), former hospital superintendent, stated that autopsies were performed in this pathology building's first floor while the lab, where histologic and microscopic preparations were done, was upstairs. Years later when this building was no longer required for use, it was used for occupational therapy and the name "Rose Cottage" was suggested by employees who didn't like the idea of working in a building that was the former morgue.

The greater majority of the original buildings that made up CLSH have been demolished. Rose Cottage is now the oldest extant building. The other remaining historic buildings include the dairy barn, also built by Mr. Carlin in 1923, and the administration building and Fuqua Hospital (1927). In 1983, Rose Cottage was entered into the National Register of Historic Buildings. Rose Cottage was converted into a mental health museum for the public to mark the centennial anniversary of the hospital. It is now known as Rose Cottage Museum.

According to the LSP website:

> (The) Rose Cottage is actually quite small, causing us to bring in only four investigators and no DVR setup. We began our investigation in the standard fashion, conducting base temperature and EMF readings. The night was fairly quiet until about 9:00 p.m. when Jennifer and Kirk were sitting downstairs in the room where the actual electroshock therapy was administered. All of a sudden, they heard an extremely loud crash, almost as if a piece of pottery had fallen from the shelf. As they got up to find the source of the noise, they noticed that an actual portion of the floor tile had literally shattered into several pieces! The loose pieces of tile that splintered off were scattered around, almost as if the tile had exploded! After numerous attempts to find an explanation for this, we were unable to come up with any logical explanations. Review of audio showed no other significant pieces of evidence. . . .

**Southern Forest Heritage Museum, 77 Longleaf Drive, Long Leaf:** According to the LSP website:

> Long Leaf is a very small town about twenty miles south of Alexandria, receiving its name from the high-quality long leaf pine that was mass-milled here. This wood produced here would be a valuable material in World War II as it was used in constructing Higgins landing craft, due to its ability to withstand the seawater. The sawmill that sits here was literally its own community, eventually becoming the town it is today. Opening in 1892, the sawmill sits on fifty-seven acres of land that also houses the buildings that were once the commissary, post office, doctor's office, Planer Mill, round house, machine shop, car knocker shed, and small homes where former employees lived with their families. . . .

The sawmill of the Long Leaf Mill is one of the oldest in the nation. The building was constructed in 1910 for the Crowell and Spencer Lumber Company (1898-1941), was remodeled in 1917 and 1936 by the Crowell Long Leaf Lumber Company (1841-1955) and renovated in the mid-1950s. By February of 1969, the last logs were cut on the long side for the Crowell Lumber Industries (1955-1969). This would be the last time any lumber passed through the sawmill at the Long Leaf Mill. The mill was officially closed in June of that year due to saw timber being no longer available.

Also noted on the LSP website:

> In the sawmill, one can find all of the standard operating equipment needed to convert logs into lumber. It is here where workers were trained to operate the then-latest in mill industrial equipment. Lumber was brought to the green train where it was sorted by grade and size and then moved to the dry kiln or was stored in the open. From there, it was moved to the Planer Mill for conversion into marketable lumber.
>
> The mill sits alongside a railway system which enabled easy transport of cut wood to its desired locations. A smaller track was built around the property to transport employees from the mill to their homes, via a small M-4 railed passenger vehicle, nicknamed the "Doodlebug" for its odd appearance. Several of the major locomotives that ran through here daily are still on the grounds. One of these engines is the hefty Crowell and Spencer #400 which operated from around 1919 until early 1953, as it continuously hauled log trains from Hutton to Long Leaf. The other significant engine here is the Meridian Lumber Company Locomotive #202 that operated during the same time as the #400, also hauling log trains on a daily basis. With its unique shape, it is known as the last example of a cabbage-stacked, wood-burning steam engine in Louisiana. . . .
>
> Another interesting piece of machinery still on the grounds is the ominous looking Clyde Rehaul Skidder. As a large tree was cut down, large hooks were fastened to the tree and with the help of an extremely powerful motor, the steel cables were reeled in along with the freshly cut pine. As one can imagine, this was a very dangerous contraption as the sudden force of the cables being pulled would often cause the hooks to dislodge from the logs, sending the heavy projectiles flying through the air at high speeds. Many a worker are said to have been killed or lost limbs because of the skidder. . . .

> Not only did you have the dangers of accidental deaths and injuries one could normally associate with a sawmill, but there were also several intentional deaths that took place here. As the mill was the primary place to work and make a living for the time, there was quite some competitiveness among workers to promote. It has been reported that on several occasions, employees were pushed off ledges in the sawmill by other staff, falling to their deaths down the deep pits. . . .
>
> In addition to the murders and accidental deaths due to the dangers of the skidder, there have been several other tragic events on the property. It is said that a young boy died after falling out the M-4 transport vehicle. Also, Engine #202 that is currently on display in the machine shop was once involved in a fatal head on collision with another train. The collision caused the boiler to rupture, literally melting the engineer!

The LSP investigators experienced much while touring Southern Forest Heritage Museum, and here are a few of their experiences:

> While sitting next to the shed that contains Engine #106, one of our investigator's jacket sleeves was forcefully tugged by an unseen force. The tug was severe enough that it actually pulled him in the opposite direction while other investigators saw him jerk. Later in the evening, while standing near the Planer Mill, the investigators heard what sounded like footsteps on the gravel. Further examination found no one present anyone around the building! Finally, while in the engine house, our members heard one of the large shed doors forcefully open and close by itself. As before, no one could be found near the site. Audio analysis proved to be equally rewarding as several interesting audio clips were recorded. . . .

## BUSINESSES

**A Commercial Building, Unstated Address, Lecompte:**
Built in the 1890s, the owners of the building did not want to share their exact location.

According to the LSP website:

> The most common report from the owner and guests is that there is often the feeling of an unseen presence. One individual reports the sighting of an unexplained mist in the air. There are also reports that not only human spirits may be present, but that there is the feeling of negative type spirit present, but this negative entity presence is supposed to have been corrected.

The LSP investigators visited on occasion, and we have spoken with the new owners of the building and they entered the building on December 19, 2015. The members of the team included: Bess Maxwell, Connie Williamson, Susan Coleman, Kirk Cormier, Keith Myers, and Traci Myers. According to the LSO report, equipment used included: Digital cameras, digital audio recorders, various EMF meters including Tri-Field, motion detectors, laser grid systems, P-SB7 spirit box, digital thermometers, infrared DVR cameras and recorder, FLIR thermal camera, ion counters, infrasound testing equipment, Ovilus interactive voice communication devices, and geophone vibration detection equipment.

According to John Combs, the leader of this group, "We, therefore, are unable to either confirm or deny the possibility of presences in the past, in the present, or the possibility of future positive findings. . . ."

**The Den, Unstated Address, Alexandria:**
According to the LSP website:

> Located in downtown Alexandria, Louisiana, The Den was built in 1896 and was used as a jewelry store and then went into disrepair. The new owner is getting the building back up to working order (as) the entire city of Alexandria is trying to revitalize the city and in the downtown area. We arrived around 7:15 p.m. and started our investigation. We were directed to the upstairs as having the most activity, so we centered around that, and we also were shown how noise was coming from the stairway and footsteps could be heard. We used our equipment, but was a quiet night, I then discovered that when the wind would blow off the main street and the Red River that the it would make noise. If you were sitting in direct relation to the office and the stairs are behind you and the window behind that, it would sound like steps from the stairwell. We then put some cardboard in the window cracks on the frame and the so-called footsteps stopped. We wrapped up investigation hours later with no

evidence and/or recordings on the real time EVP recorder. We then checked out and did a session in the kitchen area and found the table to be crooked and how stuff falls off due to it being unstable. No more evidence was found in the kitchen, and so we concluded our investigation with no verifiable validations to confirm that The Den contained any paranormal activity.

## PRIVATE RESIDENCES

**A Private Residence, Unstated Address, Pineville:**
According to the LSP website:

> We were contacted by a couple in Pineville, Louisiana, regarding their home they recently purchased only two weeks prior to contacting us. The home was estimated to have built in the late 1960s to early 1970s. Almost immediately upon moving in, the homeowners begin having strange experiences. Specifically, the owners, including their teenage daughter, all saw a strange black figure walking down the hallway. . . .
>
> We arrived at the home with a small group of four investigators and one DVR setup. After setting up our equipment, we began our investigation in the normal fashion. . . . After following up with the homeowners, they reported having no further strange activity. The one thing that is interesting to us is that the homeowner is in her last term of pregnancy and has her father's ashes stored in the home. We advised the couple that it is very possible that it could simply be the presence of her father checking in on the family. However, this cannot be validated for certain. We have offered the assistance of a Catholic priest, and the homeowners are currently considering it. . . .

**A Private Residence, Unstated Address, Deville:**
According to the LSP website:

> (LSP) Participants: Tricia Grayson, Bess Maxwell, Kirk Cormier, John Combs. The clients, husband, and wife, have lived in this home several years. The home sits on ground, in the exact spot as a prior

building. . . . In earlier years, it is possible that some individuals may have perished in this older building. The front of the current home was once a parsonage, and located on another spot. . . .

The initial activity as reported by the clients seemed to be that of a combination of activity reported as "normal haunting activity," and that which is often reported as, and attributed to, "demonic" type activity. This latter activity, by the clients' admissions, seemed to have a negative effect on their lifestyle. This, in turn, led to a crisis situation. This crisis situation caused both clients to reevaluate their current conditions, and to make positive changes. These changes included having the home blessed. At this time, the activity perceived as "demonic" ceased, but that which is normally attributed as "normal haunting activity," did not stop. . . . There have been shadow forms, cold spots, voices, household electrical devices turned off/on and interacted with, pets seeming to see/interact with persons or things not otherwise visible, water being turned on, and numerous events involving object displacement. The object displacement seems to be the largest area of activity, and involves objects moving inside the home, and some taken from the home to the outside areas. Although troubling when objects are lost, this activity does not seem to be malicious in nature. . . .

In the early evening hours, investigators Bess Maxwell and Tricia Grayson were in the master bedroom. The client (wife) had reported that, in some early morning hours, she had been awakened by the feeling that the bed was being shaken, or the sensation of an ongoing vibration. . . . Bess Maxwell was lying on the bed, as still as possible, trying to feel any type of vibration or movement of the bed. Tricia Grayson was in the room, about three feet from the foot of the bed, but at this particular moment, observing Bess Maxwell through the mirror of the dresser. Tricia thought she saw an arm (shadow form) moving in an upward direction, consistent with someone picking up or touching an object from the mattress of the bed. Just as she was asking Bess about the arm, the flashlight lying on the mattress, directly below where the arm was observed, came on without apparent human cause. The flashlight had been securely turned off, and specifically not set to come on with a slight touch or vibration, e.g., loosening the front or rear of the flashlight, in an attempt to communicate using the flashlight. . . .

> Later, in the living room, investigators Bess Maxwell and Tricia Grayson were attempting to communicate using the audio digital recorders, in gathering EVP. Just as the air-conditioning unit (central air) came on, a female voice was recorded, not otherwise heard, saying, "Turn that off now." The voice seemed agitated, or otherwise angry.
>
> If there is a presence in a home, it can sometimes not wish to interact with unknown individuals. . . . We feel that this presence is not of malicious intent. These presences seem to crave attention, and that the less attention they perceive, they more activity is generated to garner such attention. . . .

**A Boyce Residence, Unstated Address, Boyce:**
According to the LSP website:

> The clients moved into this home about two years ago. The land in the general area had belonged to another family for about one hundred years in the past, handed down from generation to generation. There are also reports of Civil War skirmishes in the general area.
>
> The clients have had experiences since moving in. They have unusual dreams, never experienced in the past. Unexplained noises are heard. Shadows are often seen, where there is no logical explanation for these to form. Strange figures have been seen in the hallway. There is often the sense or feeling of an unknown presence. The clients have had the sensation of being touched as if by unseen hands. Electrical devices are turned off and on, as if by unseen hands. Doors often seem to open and close by themselves. . . .
>
> Participants: Bess Maxwell, Connie Williamson, Kirk Cormier, and Susan Coleman. . . . Personal experiences of Bess Maxwell: Unexplained battery drains were noted in various areas of the home. Unexplained EMF spikes were noted in the back bedroom. Connie Williamson felt a distinct nudge while in The Den, as if from unseen hands. . . .
>
> Six audio clips were obtained. All were from the hallway area.
>
> Clip One: (male voice) "Get Out."
>
> Clip Two: Bess Maxwell: "Are you Robert?" Male Voice: "Yep."
>
> Clip Three: Bess Maxwell: "How did you lose your land?" Male voice: "Robert'"

Clip Four: Received as a comment. Male voice one, not clear: Male voice two, also not clear. Male voice one: "Okay!"

Clip Five: Male Voice: "Get out of the room."

Clip Six: Bess Maxwell: "How many spirits are here in the house right now?" Male voice: "Ten."

We feel that these experiences, and the positive tests received are probably indicative of an anomalous presence or presences, and that these do not seem malicious or harmful in any way. . . .

**A Private Residence, Unstated Address, Pineville:** According to the LSP website:

> The tenants that rent the building have been scratched and touched several times. Scissors and knives have been magnetized even with nothing around. Scissors have disappeared from being in the "usual spot." Also have been seeing "lights" outside the building. . . .
>
> Investigators: Grady and Brianna. . . . We had strong and strange EMF readings off a pair of common household scissors. . . . We had several personal experiences of tingles and touches. We captured an EVP of unknown knocks. Another EVP of footsteps from upstairs bedroom while in the downstairs living room. A third EVP of an unexplained dragging noise. Also captured were nine unexplained orbs. These were so numerous that I am not going to try and list all of them, but they are seen in the video evidence with this report. . . . In regard to the private residence in Pineville, LA, we strongly feel activity is prevalent here. . . .

**A Private Residence, Unstated Address, Pineville:** According to the LSP website:

> Owners have been experiencing noises, such as talking and humming coming from the upstairs area of the home. There is no one that goes up there except to go to the restroom. Owner also states that while he is there by himself, he will talk to a woman that is humming and has seen things move. There has also been knocking on walls and floors and even went so far as to jump on the top floor and move the chandelier on the bottom floor ceiling. There have been reports about hangers moving in the upstairs closets. The lady of the house hates going upstairs and is afraid of a room that a previous person

> lived in and keeps the door shut. They were also recording on their own and said that the recorder was cut off and back on again with a four minute gap or so in between the recordings and that the recorder moved also from the spot that it was placed. The lady also stated that she feels like she will be pushed down the stairs and she goes down sideways hanging on to the rails for support so as the "person" won't push her down the stairs. . . .
>
> Investigators: Grady, Bree, Christy, Harv. . . . We did capture several pieces of evidence in the house (including) an unexplained voice on the spirit box in one of the kid's rooms upstairs saying, "Do what." One of our deer cams while we were setting up caught another unexplained voice in a different upstairs bedroom saying, "Yay." We also captured several EVPs in the home including a, "Hey," something that sounds like, "Her," and a few unidentified words. Also captured were some very awesome orbs on our cameras. . . .
>
> In regard to the private residence in Pineville, LA, we strongly feel activity is prevalent here. . . .

The LSP group is not only an amazing organization, but each member is also amazing and talented. Keep up the good work!

# Other Central Louisiana Spirited Places

## "The Spirit World Is Alive and Well in Cenla!"

There are dozens of spirited places throughout Central Louisiana along with the previously mentioned sites in Rapides Parish. Here is a summary guide to some of the major and most interesting sites. The following quotes come from several sources including: the Alexandria *Town Talk* newspaper, TT; Ghosts of America, GA; Louisiana Spirits Paranormal investigators, LSP; *Haunted Nation, HN; Weird Louisiana, WL;* or the author's personal interviews and investigations, PI):

**Allen Parish:**
There are several ghost stories listed for this parish on the Ghosts of America website, including stories on (with at least one sighting): Elizabeth, Grant, Kinder, Oberlin, and Reeves.

Town(s) with at least three sightings: Oakdale

**Avoyelles Parish:**
There are several ghost stories listed for this parish on the Ghosts of America website, including stories on (with at least one sighting): Bunkie, Center Point, Effie, Evergreen, Hamburg, Hessmer, Mansura, Marksville, Moreauville, Plaucheville, and Simmesport.

Town(s) with at least two sightings: Cottonport.

Here are additional Avoyelles sites with brief descriptions:

**Former Bailey's Theater (demolished), 120 West Oak Street, Bunkie (TT)**

**Fort DeRussy and Fort DeRussy Cemetery, off LA Highway 1192 outside of Marksville:**
"If you dare. Near the Fort DeRussy Civil War battlefield, the site is the final resting spot for the soldiers who fell during the battle and reportedly also for a witch who was buried outside of the fence surrounding the cemetery." *(TT)*

**Old (Auguste) Voinche Building, South Washington Street, Marksville (LSP)**

**Bailey's Theater/Bar, 113 East Ogden Street, Courthouse Square in Marksville (LSP)**

**The Woods outside of Marksville, outside of Marksville:**
"Marksville has its own haunted woods along the Red River. Many witnesses have sworn that they have seen headless men marching among the trees. Supposedly, these were the soldiers that fought a battle, and the dead were buried in a long trench." *(TT)*

**A Private Residence, Marksville (LSP)**

**Sacred Heart Catholic Church Cemetery, 9986 Bayou Des Glaises Street, Moreauville:**
Felix Moncla was twenty-seven years old when he and his copilot disappeared without a trace, along with their US Air Force jet airplane. The jet was sent to respond to a mysterious radar blip. The plaque on his memorial reads, "Disappeared November 23, 1953, Intercepting a UFO Over Canadian Border."

According to a front-page article of the December 19, 1953 edition of the *Weekly News* of Marksville:

> Lt. Felix E. "Gene" Moncla Presumed Lost in Jet Crash
>
> Presumed dead in the crash of an F89-C in Lake Superior is First Lieutenant Felix E. Moncla, known to his friends and family as "Gene." The jet he was piloting disappeared while he was on a mission from Kinross air base, Sault Ste. Marie, Michigan. The accident occurred on Monday, November 23, and this week, more

> than three weeks later, his brave mother, Mrs. Moncla Sr., known to the Avoyelles people as the former Yvonne Beridon, has not given up hope. Tuesday afternoon, she declared that it was "a mother who held out-through hope and prayer-until the last." Her eyes dimmed with tears as she spoke of her only son; of his plans to continue his medical studies when he would be released from air force duties. She spoke of his fine wife, the former Miss Bobbie Jean Coleman of Waco, Texas, and of the couple's little son, David Carl, two years, and of their baby daughter, Sharon Yvonne, almost eight months. Mrs. Moncla tightened her lips and heaved a deep sigh, and then a faint smile wreathed her face, and she said, "Who knows, he could be back for Christmas."
>
> The air force has not declared that Lt. Moncla is dead, just missing.
>
> At the time that the young pilot and his radio observer, Second Lt. Robert L. Wilson, took off to investigate an unidentified flying object, their jet had two hours of fuel and was equipped with rubber rafts. Each of the lieutenants wore a life jacket. . . .

Wilson's body was found, but Moncla's body disappeared and was never found. . . .

**Beauregard Parish:**
There are several ghost stories listed for this parish on the Ghosts of America website, including stories on (with at least one sighting): Dry Creek, Merryville, Ragley, and Sugartown.

Town(s) with at least two sightings: Longville.

Town(s) with at least five sightings: DeRidder.

**Old Beauregard Parish Jail also known as The DeRidder Gothic Jail, 205 West First Street, DeRidder:**
The jail is one of the most interesting buildings on this side of the state, closing in 1984 as it was considered a health hazard. The jail, opened in 1914, is connected to the next door courthouse by an underground tunnel. This unique Gothic-style building is known locally as the "hanging jail" because a double execution took place there in 1928. The jail is often used as a haunted house at Halloween time.

On March 9, 1928, Molton "Mosey" Brasseaux and Joe Genna were both executed for the murder of forty-five-year old local taxi cab driver Joseph Brevelle. Just after noon, they walked up the spiral staircase and one at a time plunged three levels down breaking their necks. There are reports that the two killers never left the jail, at least in spirit. Reports of strange evanescent figures have been seen by numerous witnesses. The spirits lurk around the solitary confinement prison cells that the two men were kept in, the cells adjacent to the hanging chamber.

**Caldwell Parish:**
There are several ghost stories listed for this parish on the Ghosts of America website, including stories on (with at least one sighting): Columbia, Grayson, and Kelly.

**Catahoula Parish:**
There are several ghost stories listed for this parish on the Ghosts of America website, including stories on (with at least one sighting): Aimwell, Enterprise, Harrisonburg, Jonesville, and Sicily Island.

**Concordia Parish:**
There are several ghost stories listed for this parish on the Ghosts of America website, including stories on (with at least one sighting): Acme, Clayton, Ferriday, Monterey, and Wildsville.

Town(s) with at least two sightings: Vidalia.

**Frogmore Cotton Plantation and Gins, 11656 US Highway 84, Frogmore, near Ferriday:**
"In the 1940s, the Sojourners lived in the house along with the ghosts. Once Mrs. Boyd Sojourner saw a man dressed in a white suit walk across the hallway from a bedroom toward what is now the parlor. He then disappeared. She clearly saw him across the twelve-foot-wide hallway before this figure dissolved before her eyes.

"Around 1951, Jack Ellard and his family were living in the main house and one day he was standing outside of the house with his daughter. He and the little girl saw a woman, all dressed in black with a veil, standing pensively by one of the columns of the house. He told the child not to be frightened as it was her mother. As he was uttering these reassuring words, the woman in black abruptly vanished. He ran into the house where his wife was sitting and asked her why she had scared them like that. She insisted that she hadn't been outside.

"The mysterious woman in black was not the only encounter with the unknown Mr. Ellard experienced. Regularly, the lights in the bedroom flashed on and off by themselves. He heard chains rattling in one of the back bedrooms, which was always kept locked. On three occasions he saw the front doorknob turn and the door swing open, letting in only the night. This door has the original carpenter lock that dates to the building of the house in 1815. It is operated by a long skeleton key and remains the only way to lock the house to this day. Another time the clock strangely rang at three o'clock. Normally, this would not be an odd experience except that the clock has not been wound in years. (Mr. Ellard speculates that it has been at least fifty years since it was wound), and the clock actually struck the correct hour. Since this bizarre occurrence, the clock has remained silent.

"Despite sharing his home with ghosts, Mr. Ellard took comfort in the fact that they were friendly ghosts and they did not seem to bother his family except for some small unexplained events. Everyday realty was disrupted just slightly by these ghosts as they ventured away from their eternal abode." (*Louisiana's Haunted Plantations,* Jill Pascoe)

**Desoto Parish:**

There are several ghost stories listed for this parish on the Ghosts of America website, including stories on (with at least one sighting): Frierson, Gloster, Grand Cane, Mansfield, Many, Pelican, and Stonewall.

Town(s) with at least four sightings: Keachi.

Town(s) with at least eleven sightings: Logansport.

**Evangeline Parish:**

There are several ghost stories listed for this parish on the Ghosts of America website, including stories on (with at least one sighting): Basile, Chataignier, Mamou, Pine Prairie, Reddell,. St. Landry, and Turkey Creek.

Town(s) with at least two sightings: Ville Platte.

**Franklin Parish:**

There are several ghost stories listed for this parish on the Ghosts of America website, including stories on (with at least one sighting): Fort Necessity, Mangham, and Winnsboro.

Town(s) with at least two sightings: Gilbert.

Town(s) with at least five sightings: Baskin.

Town(s) with at least six sightings: Wisner.

**The Former Green Light Bridge, Green Light Road, Off LA Highway 15, south of Winnsboro:**

"(This is) where legend says an eerie, ghostly, green light has been seen on the bridge and the banks of the creek. . . .

"'It was a really cool, old, wooden bridge,' says Paul Price of Franklin Parish. 'It didn't have any sides. . . . I saw the light, but it didn't scare me or anything. I haven't thought about that place in years.'

"'Isaac Eley said, "Just across the bridge, there was an old, old church built in the late 1800s. . . . The story goes that someone was hung at the tree at the church.' Ely speaks about another incident in almost the same place, in front of the church, 'There was a lady that got killed years ago, at least in the '50s or '60s. She was killed in an automobile accident right there at the church. I believe she ran into a tree.'

"Louis Robinson of Winnsboro confirmed Eley's story, 'I'm forty-five and this happened years before I was born. There was a hanging at the church. The church was just west of the (Green Light) bridge. . . . There was a lady who did have a wreck at the church. She said she saw a ghost and had a wreck and later died.'" (*TT)*

**Grant Parish:**

There are several ghost stories listed for this parish on the Ghosts of America website, including stories on (with at least one sighting): Bentley, Colfax, Dry Prong, Georgetown,. Montgomery, and Pollock.

Pollock Town Hall, Pollock (TT, LSP)

**Big Creek Cemetery, Dyson Creek Road, Pollock:**

"This cemetery is said to be very active by local paranormal groups who claim to have captured numerous photographic anomalies and EVPs here." (hauntedplaces.org)

**Historical Jail, Faircloth and Fourth Streets, Colfax:**

"We are a local paranormal research team filming and investigating places for the brand-new TV series called *True Ghost Stories.* Upon our scouting and places to film and investigate for the show, we ran across the well-known and documented place in Colfax Louisiana called The Colfax Riot of 1873, which has a very bloody history. After all research was done, we finally went in to investigate. The history there is still very much alive and active as we caught everything from shadows to disembodied voices and several other strange phenomena." (hauntedplaces.org)

**LaSalle Parish:**
There are several ghost stories listed for this parish on the Ghosts of America website, including stories on (with at least one sighting): Olla, Trout, Tullos, and Urania.

Town(s) with at least three sightings: Jena.

**Natchitoches Parish:**
There are several ghost stories listed for this parish on the Ghosts of America website, including stories on (with at least one sighting): Ashland, Campti, Clarence, Goldonna, Marthaville, Melrose, Mora, Natchez, Powhatan, Provencal, and Robeline.

Town(s) with at least two sightings: Cloutierville and Gorum.

Town(s) with at least three sightings: Natchitoches.

**"Bigfoot" Sightings near Goldonna. (PI)**
**"Plantation Treasures," 720 Front Street, Natchitoches (LSP)**

**Old Courthouse Museum, 600 Second Street, Natchitoches:**
"It carries its own haunted tales of hangings in the street and faces of the condemned." *(TT)* As is noted, many convicts over the decades used to be hung in this courthouse.

**Natchitoches American Cemetery, Second Street STE 200, Natchitoches**
"There the legend of a grave inside a tree speaks of ghostly images and the specter of an Indian princess." *(TT)*

**Northwestern State University, 175 Sam Sibley Drive, Natchitoches:**
"Isabella, the woman in a glowing white gown has been seen on the NSU campus. She was first seen in East Hall which was torn down in 1932, then she moved on to Caldwell Hall, which burned in 1982. She was next spotted in the women's gymnasium in which also burned a few years ago, and these days she is sometimes spotted in Varnado Hall." *(TT)*

**Cherokee Plantation, 3109 LA Highway 494, Natchitoches (along the Cane River):**
". . . is said to have its own ghost as well." *(TT)*

**The former Kate Chopin House, formerly called The Bayou Folk Museum (no longer exists), LA State Highway 495, Cloutierville:** "The odor was strong, so strong that she might still can smell it. Candles. They were burning in the upstairs parlor. 'And, they weren't any candles,' Maybell Carter said. 'There weren't any candles to be found anywhere.'

"Sudden silence. The thought of it as is strong as the odor. No candles, but a smoky smell. 'And I'll always remember it,' Maybell said. 'Until this day, I'll remember it.'

"That was Alexis Cloutier's third appearance. He showed up the first time long before Amanda Chennault was named curator of the Kate Chopin House. And the Chopin House seems to stand in Haunt Central. Well maybe it's not that bad. . . . The Chopin House could be considered one of these old homes, but its ghost didn't appear until long after Lyle Saxon patronized the place. . . ." *(TT)*

**Monett's Ferry Crossing Over Cane River, at the intersection with LA Highway 1 with LA Highway 490, Natchitoches Parish:**

This was the scene of the Civil War Battle of Monett's Ferry. "Legend has it that cars stall in and around that area where LA Highway 1 passes the Monett's Ferry site." *(TT)*

**Lacey Branch, (no directions available), Natchitoches:**
"'At Lacey Branch, near Natchitoches, there is a headless horseman who rides about the road, frightening motorists and late pedestrians,' writes the late author Lyle Saxon. 'The story of his origin seems to be unknown, which makes him all the more awesome, since to understand what some of these phantoms are about partially alleviates the terror of the person who meets them.'

"'I remember hearing stories of the headless horseman when I was growing up,' Lena Allbritton of Robeline said to the *Town Talk* newspaper. . . . He supposedly roams a few miles south of Fort Jessup State Historic Site. 'And people living around that area a long time ago have told stories about hearing chains rattling at milking time,' she said. 'Milking time was right when it started getting dark. They'd go out and milk their cows. The chains would rattle, but no one would ever show up.'" *(TT)*

**Simmons House, 219 Williams Avenue, Natchitoches:**
". . . an old two-story dwelling, with the usual or plain ghost type, who raps on walls and rattles chains. . . " *(TT)*

**The Arglefargin, near Johnson's Chute, Natchitoches:**
"In the *Old Natchitoches Parish Magazine*, reporter Bob Norman described a bizarre series of disappearances near Johnson's Chute, along the Cane River Bottoms. These nineteenth-century mysteries were generally attributed to a monster known as the *arglefargin.*

"Beginning in the 1860s, you men in the area would occasionally go missing. When their whereabouts were traced from the sites where they had last been seen, searchers would often come upon a violent struggle. Along with scuffed earth and broken branches, they'd find huge monsterlike footprints mingled with the tracks of the missing youths. Occasionally, they'd often come upon a mysterious word—*arglefargi*n or *argilfirkin*—scrawled on a note pinned to a tree or scratched into the dry mud with a sharp stick. For a long time no one knew what this meant.

"The hunt for the *arglefargi*n was on. Farmers set traps baited with full-size farm animals but caught only ordinary predators like bears or panthers. When a local savant named Mrs. Jane came up with a novel explanation for the missing men, claiming 'the people were being abducted by creatures from the moon to be used as slave labor.' This was a little hard to believe so one young man of spirit offered himself as bait for the traps. After days in the back country, he emerged exhausted, with the details of the truth. The *arglefargi*n, he said, were not from the moon, but were humanoids who stood roughly nine and eleven feet tall and looked "Something like a cross between the ugliest person who ever lived, a mutant gorilla, and a hackberry with Dutch elm disease.' They also smelled like dead skunks and had a strong desire to mate. . . . According to the local lore that emerged following Mrs. Janes's human-baited trap, *arglefargi*n were a long-lost branch from the human family tree. Their own species had gone into decline due to their size and low birth rate, and so they were attempting to reinvigorate the species bloodline with new generic material from human male Louisianans. . . ." (*Weird Louisiana)*

**The Headless Woman, near Natchitoches:**
"In the 1920s, a woman (who didn't work for the railroad) was riding the train from Coushatta to Natchitoches. Her destination: speakeasy far from the town she lived in where she could consume an illegal amount of alcohol . . . in those days of Prohibition. . . . Our heroine spent the larger part of the evening at the speakeasy. . . . Soon after boarding, she fell off the platform at the rear of the car and had her head torn off. Ever since that evening, the ghost of the ill-fated flapper has been spotted on (LA) Highway 480 between Coushatta and Campti." (*Weird Louisiana)*

**Magnolia Plantation, 5776 LA Highway 119, Derry:**
"The 1830 Magnolia Plantation has a main plantation house, slaves' quarters, store, blacksmith shop, and slave hospital. The site, built by Ambrose Lecomte II and his wife Julia Buard, is now owned by the National Park Service and is believed to be haunted by mistreated slaves. Reports say that the plantation's slaves were punished using leg stocks and starvation and were crowded into tiny living spaces. Rumor has it that the slaves used voodoo to curse their masters, as is evident in the enslaved blacksmiths' crosses over the family's graves—West African voodoo symbols are hidden within the design. Witnesses to the supernatural activity here say apparitions have been seen, motion detectors go off for no reason, and disembodied voices can be heard." (hauntedplaces.org)

**St. Maurice Plantation, Mansion Road, St. Maurice:**
"It is said that the ghost of a child comes from the cemetery and visits the manor home, making sudden noises or rushing past. He also likes to change the pages on the calendar. He is believed to have started the fire that burned the mansion down in 1980." (hauntedplaces.org)

**Red River Parish:**
There are several ghost stories listed for this parish on the Ghosts of America website, including stories on (with at least one sighting): Coushatta and Hall Summit.

**Sabine Parish:**
There are several ghost stories listed for this parish on the Ghosts of America website, including stories on (with at least one sighting): Converse, Fisher, Florien, Many, Noble, and Pleasant Hill.

Town(s) with at least two sightings: Belmont and Zwolle.

Town(s) with at least three sightings: Hornbeck.

**St. Landry Parish:**
There are several ghost stories listed for this parish on the Ghosts of America website, including stories on (with at least one sighting): Arnaudville, Grand Coteau, Krotz Springs, Lawtell, Lebeau, Melville, Morrow, Palmetto, Port Barre, and Sunset.

Town(s) with at least two sightings: Opelousas.

Town(s) with at least three sightings: Washington.

**Chretien Point, 665 Chretien Point Road, Sunset:**
From the Chretien Point website:

"The Deep South's most intriguing plantation mansion is just fourteen miles north of Lafayette. You can spend hours exploring this historic columned home built in 1831 and set on twenty secluded acres on the banks of the Bayou Bourbeaux.

"The mansion was the center of a thriving three-thousand-acre cotton plantation with five hundred slaves in its heyday. The centerpiece twelve-room red brick mansion itself is spectacular with a rich history of former tenants. The most noteworthy of which is Jean Lafitte, a flamboyant gambler. His equally flamboyant widow smoked cigars and doubled her husband's fortune.

"Many people have reported seeing ghosts throughout the years. There are also tales of buried treasure on the grounds.

"Civil War battles were fought on the property. A Union cannonball destroyed the uppermost section of the westernmost column of the house and there is still a bullet hole on one of the front doors.

"The famous staircase in the movie *Gone with the Wind* where Scarlett O'Hara shoots a pillaging Union soldier was a replica of Chretien Point mansion stairway."

As reported by the Alexandria *Town Talk* newspaper:

"'The bridge (Marland's Bridge, located on the way to Chretien Point) by this plantation is incredible. You can hear voices, marching boots and on one occasion we got run off by a strong sulfur smell,' said Toni Daigle in a 2015 post on hauntedplaces.org. 'As soon as we moved from the bridge, the smell was gone. . . .'

"In March of this year (2015), an anonymous writer said: 'We came at night to see if we could see ghosts. We were parked on the bridge. Her car would not start. She (tried and tried), but it wouldn't start. I told her to push the truck off the bridge. So she did. Then the truck started right up.'"

Another report:

"(Chretien Point is) reportedly haunted by the ghost of its former mistress as well as an outlaw she killed when she discovered him creeping up the stairs one night." (hauntedplaces.org)

**Nicholson House, LA Highway 182 and Vine Street, Opelousas:**
"Thought to be over 250 years old, the building was once used as a Civil War hospital. It is haunted by a ghost called Hoppy or Peg-Leg, seen wearing soldier's clothing, a peg-leg, and a gold earring in his left ear. Legend has it

that Hoppy was a pirate who was captured and turned traitor to his fellows. He lost his leg in battle and eventually died of gangrene. In addition to seeing his apparition, witnesses have reported hearing his footsteps, including the tapping of his peg-leg, at around sunset." (hauntedplaces.org)

**Saint Charles Borromeo Retreat House, 214 Church Street, Grand Coteau:**
"Rumor has it that this house is haunted by an old Jesuit priest who used to live there." (hauntedplaces.org)

**Eunice Public Library, 222 South Second Street, Eunice:**
"Eunice Public Library is believed to have a ghost who locks doors, turns on lights, and hides books by local children's author Mary Alice Fontenot." (hauntedplaces.org)

**Vernon Parish:**
There are several ghost stories listed for this parish on the Ghosts of America website, including stories on (with at least one sighting): Evans, Hornbeck, New Llano, Pitkin, Rosepine, and Simpson.

Town(s) with at least two sightings: Anacoco.

Town(s) with at least nine sightings: Leesville

**Smythe Residence, Unstated Address, Leesville (LSP)**

**Fort Johnson (formerly Fort Polk), 1591 Bell Richard Avenue, Leesville:**
There are twenty-four ghost stories listed for Fort Johnson on the Ghosts of America website; here is a small sampling of them:

"I was a janitor, and we used to clean a building that was the old South Fort emergency room that is now being used for a child development center on Utah Avenue. I had always heard of the haunting there. They said a young boy, no more than seven years old, roamed the place in the evening. I did in fact encounter the little boy on several different occasions. He would knock over our brooms, open our doors, and put handprints on windows that we just cleaned. They were just mischievous things a boy his age would typically do.

"I saw him at the end of a spooky hallway one night, and around the same time letters on a bulletin board rearranged themselves to spell PARADOX! I felt like something was following me every time I worked in that building to the point that I refused to enter it alone. One night I was heading up the hallway because I had to get some extra cleaning supplies, and I saw the black figure that was childlike walk down the hallway toward me. It then went through the wall and out onto the playground equipment. That was enough for me to say out loud the crossing over ritual that was intended on safe cross over to the other side, and/or if it was Satan that it was compelled by the blood of Christ to leave us alone and do our job. I never saw the little boy again. Either he was crossed over, or he was Satan masquerading.

"A year or so rolled by, and I was working another job coming home late one night. I decided to do a pass by the building, and lo and behold I saw a man-like figure looking out of the window almost as if to say there was a lot of paranormal activity going on in this building. I mean from what I know, it was a defunct hospital that may have even had a morgue in it. Literally many people came here to die. I have worked in several other buildings on the base, and I have never encountered anything as unsettling as that.

"One of my coworkers even dubbed it the "booger-building" in reference to the paranormal activity that took place in that particular building. I was also tempted through a telepathic brainwave mechanism to almost go down a corridor where the trauma patients were taken to. Talk about a tough mental fight with something that has rearranged letters to spell a message out (Paradox) and was trying to lead me down the corridor of advanced darkness. I never ventured down it. Eventually I left that occupation because of the intrusive thoughts that accompanied me when I worked in that building. My suggestion is that definitely be blessed up if you dare go to this building."

"We were stationed at Fort Polk in 1993 to 1997. We lived on Cline Court. Back then these were older quad-duplex homes. At the time we had two boys who were three and four. One night my husband had to work a mid-shift. This would be the first time we would experience something there. When my husband worked mid-shifts, I usually slept on the couch. I would watch a movie, so I could fall asleep. I was a very light sleeper, especially when he wasn't home. That night my oldest son had fallen asleep at my feet on the other end of the couch. I had fallen asleep facing the back of the couch.

"At some point during the wee hours of the morning I woke up with the feeling that one of my kiddos were standing over me looking at me. I could feel that presence close to my face, so I turned back to look, and there was nothing. I looked down by my feet, and my son was still sleeping. I looked around a little more to make sure my other son wasn't awake, and he was still in bed. I shrugged it off, turned back over and fell back to sleep.

"After a little while, I woke back up to that same feeling. I turned around, and again there was nothing. My boys were still asleep. I decided to just watch some TV. After a few minutes my son, who was sleeping at my feet, woke up because he needed to use the bathroom. The light switch to the hall light was in the living room, and we also left the dim light in the bathroom on for him.

"As he approached the hallway, he paused, then screamed. I got up quickly to see what was wrong, and he then told me a little girl had scared him. I ran into their room to check on the two-year-old, and he was still asleep. It confirmed what I kept feeling. It felt as if it was one of my kids trying to wake me up. I brought my other son to the living room and stayed awake the rest of the time till my hubby got home.

"After that, the boys would go off. At night it sounded as if somebody walked past the closet where the air-conditioning unit was at. We just tried to keep it normal. We didn't feed into it and just prayed for our home. All we could do. Funny (that) I found this site. I've always continued to wonder if anyone else experienced stuff in that same unit or elsewhere on Fort Polk (now Fort Johnson). . . ." (GA)

**Anacoco Woods, Anacoco:**

"I grew up in Anacoco. I spent many years there just riding my bike or walking the wooded trails. There is a section of the woods near the house where I grew up. My friends and I used to explore them. Heck, we even built many forts in there. In one spot, there was an old tree that someone scratched the name 'Alex' into. We used that tree as a base for one of our many forts.

"The third day we were hanging out there when it got dark. My friend had a flashlight on his bike, so we weren't too worried about staying there. That is until we heard the crying. It was with us this crying sound. We could all hear it. This child was crying. Chris called out to it. We heard hard breathing. It was almost as though someone breathed in shock. Then a giggle. We got on our bikes and left. The next day we purposely stayed late to hear the sound again. No cries this time. As the sun went down, all of our bikes fell over. We heard a faint giggle, then silence again." (GA)

**Winn Parish:**

There are several ghost stories listed for this parish on the Ghosts of America website, including stories on (with at least one sighting): Atlanta, Calvin, Dodson, and Sikes.

Town(s) with at least seven sightings: Winnfield.

# BIGFOOT

## "WHO IS THAT WALKING OVER THERE?"

Every day, new species of creatures are found somewhere in the world. This also applies to Central Louisiana. One purported new species that has been frequently talked about around the world and in Cenla too is Bigfoot. He goes by many names but is also commonly known as Sasquatch. He is a large and hairy human-like mythical creature alleged by some to inhabit forests in North America, particularly in the Pacific Northwest. Since the mid-twentieth century, Bigfoot has grown into a cultural icon, permeating popular culture and becoming the subject of its own distinct subculture.

Enthusiasts of Bigfoot, such as those within the pseudoscience of cryptozoology, have offered various forms of dubious evidence to prove Bigfoot's existence, including anecdotal claims of sightings as well as alleged photographs, video and audio recordings, hair samples, and casts of large footprints. However, the scientific consensus is that Bigfoot, and alleged evidence, is a combination of folklore, misidentification, and hoax rather than a living animal.

Bigfoot is often described as a large, muscular, and bipedal human or ape-like creature covered in black, dark brown, or dark reddish hair. Anecdotal descriptions estimate a height of roughly six to nine feet (1.8–2.7 m), with some descriptions having the creatures standing as tall as ten to fifteen feet (3.0–4.6 m). Some alleged observations describe Bigfoot as more human than ape, particularly regarding the face. In 1971, multiple people in The

Dalles, Oregon filed a police report describing an "overgrown ape," and one of the men claimed to have sighted the creature in the scope of his rifle but could not bring himself to shoot it because "it looked more human than animal."

Common descriptions include broad shoulders, no visible neck, and long arms, which many skeptics attribute to misidentification of a bear standing upright. Some alleged nighttime sightings have stated the creature's eyes "glowed" yellow or red. However, eyeshine is not present in humans or any other known great apes, and so proposed explanations for observable "eyeshine" off the ground in the forest include owls, raccoons, or opossums perched in foliage.

Mrs. Douglas (Shirley Bell) Rasberry of Goldonna, Natchitoches Parish, in Central Louisiana may have seen Bigfoot. She gives one of the most credible sighting reports ever given in Central Louisiana to me. Shirley gave me the following report recently:

> In the spring of 2016, I was raising two grandchildren at my home. We were on the back deck one morning. I had bought some plants and was teaching my grandchildren how to plant.
>
> I smelled this truly horrible smell. It was like old roadkill. We continued to plant the flowers. This was the day that I saw him. We have a pond behind our house. He came out on the left side (of the pond area). I asked the girls if they smelled that horrible smell, and they said yes. It smelled truly horrible. He came out of the woods, this strange thing. (He was) Like nine feet tall. We later measured from the tree limbs how tall he was. He was hairy all over and was big, humongous. The girls saw it. One of them began screaming. I had to put my hand over her mouth. He turned halfway and looked at us. The girls kept screaming. I didn't know what this thing was. I just knew it wasn't supposed to be there. The female (Bigfoot) came out from the right side (of the pond). I could tell she was a female because she had big boobs. She went straight back to the back of the property, and soon both were gone for good.

There are many reports here locally of Bigfoot, some questionable, others the witnesses didn't want to report. But all of these people had no connection to each other, lived in different locales, but all had similar reports. There is something, possibly even more than one thing, out there in the woods. And no one ever wants to meet him, or her, up close.

Here is another great story on Bigfoot, this one from the Boggy Bayou Bigfoot in Rapides Parish:

> On August 29, 2000, the *Alexandria Town Talk* reported a major sighting by two loggers near Cotton Island, east of Esler Regional Airport in Northeast Rapides Parish. According to an article by Andrew Griffin, on August 22 log foreman Earl Whitstine was removing hardwood logs using a tree cutter when he spotted a mysterious creature that he later referred to as a "booger." The beast, which he described as being about seven feet tall, covered in black hair, with big feet, appeared to be startled by the loud noise of the tree cutter. It leaped up and waded across the creek before disappearing in the woods. "After it jumped into the water, it looked back at me," he said.
>
> A few days later, Whitstine was with saw-cutter Carl Michael Dubois when the pair spotted the large-footed beast as they were walking along Boggy Bayou at the edge of Mary Ward's wooded property. This time Whitstine shouted at it, but the creature ran away before they could approach. The men then discovered a series of huge four-toed tracks in the muddy bottom of the dry bayou. They measured the stride at about six and a half feet between the tracks.
>
> Mrs. Ward was alerted to the strange discovery on her land, and sheriff's deputies soon joined her at the edge of the bayou where they could see giant footprints extending thirty feet before disappearing, thanks to the harder-packed soil in the woods.
>
> As word of the sightings spread around town, curiosity seekers flocked to Ward's property. Bigfoot researcher Scott Kessler of Pineville arrived on the scene and made plaster casts of several of the Boggy Bayou tracks and collected a number of hair samples before the invasion of onlookers could destroy all of the evidence. After several hundred visitors had swarmed over the premises, Mrs. Ward erected a sign that read:
>
> BIGFOOT PROTECTION AREA—ROAD IS CLOSED TO PUBLIC
>
> Although she continued to allow anyone without guns or dogs to explore her property as long as they agreed not to harm the

beast. Eventually, according to the sheriff's report filed later, she even began selling t-shirts and tickets to visitors.

A few days later, fisherman Larry Satcher came forward with a story about a "hairy fella" he had seen a few months earlier while casting for bass at the Honey Hole Slough on another part of Ward's acreage. As Andrew Griffin's follow-up article in the *Town Talk* described it, Satcher detected a strong pungent smell while fishing. As he waded out in the slough to cast his lure, he heard a noise and turned in time to see a pack of feral hogs on the bank. And then, he saw *it*—seven feet tall, covered with dark mottled hair, tucking a 150-pound hog under its arm as though it were a ladies' pocketbook.

"When I finally got out of the water, I started to run," he said, but when he looked back to see it was gaining on him, the creature had already disappeared. Even so, he said, "I ran as fast as I could and even passed my truck. . . . I was scared so bad."

The Honey Hole Slough is only a few hundred yards from Boggy Bayou, so in all likelihood the three eyewitnesses had seen the same creature. "I don't know if it was Bigfoot or whatever (but) if it had wanted to catch me, it could have caught me," Satcher said. "It definitely will stay with me for the rest of my life."

After Satcher's Honey Hole encounter, Mary Ward began avoiding the most thickly wooded parts of her land. Her faith in the existence of the animal remained unshaken even after forensic anthropologists and veterinary pathologists at Louisiana State University in Baton Rouge determined that the hair samples that Scott Kessler had collected at the site had come from a horse. Another scientist at Oregon National Primate Research Center had reported that the hair samples had come from a cow. Still, Ward didn't doubt the eyewitness accounts, and Bigfoot researcher Kessler was quick to point out that the presence of domestic livestock hair on the scene didn't mean that a Bigfoot hadn't also been there.

So Ward continued to believe in the existence of her Boggy Bayou Bigfoot. "I'm a little uneasy," she said, "I don't think it'd hurt me, but I know it's there now." (*Weird Louisiana*)

# A Central Louisiana Ghost Story

## "More Truth Than Fiction"

Sylvia Yancy Davis of Alexandria is one of the premier story tellers in Louisiana and beyond. A resident of Alexandria, she is the Catholic diocese superintendent of schools there. Although she has told her ghost stories all her life to thousands of eager listeners, she has never before shared one to be published. This is her first published story:

### The Single Red Rose

"Hey Bae! Let's go on a cruise!"

"Man, you're crazy. That's too much water to drink."

That was the conversation that she and her husband had at least monthly for fifty years. They were kids when they met. She was going to be a senior in high school, and he was entering his second year of college.

She was a part of a new program at the university that afforded high school seniors to earn college credit the summer before receiving their high school diplomas. Since the program was new, no one at the university suspected that the twelve eager "freshmen" weren't yet high school graduates. She met him during her second week of the eight-week program. An older friend from her hometown, whom she trusted completely, set her up on a blind date. It was on that occasion when she also met the blind date's roommate. The blind date was much too aggressive for her taste, so needless to say, it didn't work out. The roommate, however, was quieter, with a sly smile, and he was possibly the best-looking thing she had ever seen. "Why, oh why, couldn't he have been the blind date?" The evening ended, and she was disappointed.

The following night she was studying in her room when a call came that she had a gentleman caller downstairs in the lobby. At that time, men were not allowed in ladies' dormitory rooms, and they were only allowed in the lobby at certain times. All ladies had a curfew, and rooms were checked to ensure that they were tucked in safely and securely. She couldn't imagine who in the world would be calling because the date last night didn't go well, and she didn't really know any other gentlemen. When she got to the lobby, she heard a voice say, "Hey! It's me. I'm the caller." She turned to see the roommate smiling that sly smile.

That was the beginning of an incredible summer romance. If they weren't in class or studying, they spent most of their evenings together. Since neither of them had much money, their evenings were simple. They would often eat popcorn and drink cokes in the park or take a leisurely stroll around the campus. They just enjoyed each other's company. When the summer session was ending, he told her that he had previously thought about taking a year off from college to work, but after meeting her, he couldn't wait to return in the fall. It was then that she had to tell him the truth about her status. She wouldn't be on campus in the fall. She had to return to her hometown to finish high school. He was completely surprised. "How old are you?"

"Sixteen."

"Lord, I'm twenty. I'm going to jail."

She laughed. "You've had a birthday this year. I haven't. And as soon as I finish high school, I'll be back."

"And when you come back, I'll be waiting. And I'm going marry you."

And he did.

They were just kids, married, and thinking they could survive off love alone. They had a lot to learn. He never returned to college, but she did. He was the breadwinner, and she would come home every weekend to their modest apartment. They struggled, but they were happy. On their first Valentine's Day together, he bought her a single red rose. It was all he could afford. "It's to remind my valentine of my love forever. Wish we could go on a cruise too."

"Man, not a cruise. That's too much water to drink."

It wasn't very long before there was an addition to this family. They struggled even more, but they were happy.

She earned her college degree and started to work. Now she was home all the time, and being a married couple with a family was real. The bills were real. Taking care of a baby was real. Cooking and housekeeping were real. They still struggled, but they were happy. . . *most* of the time. But happy or not, he still remembered that single red rose every Valentine's Day. And he'd always say that it was to remind his valentine of his love forever. And he'd always add, "We ought to go on a cruise."

And her response was always the same, "Man, not a cruise. That's too much water to drink."

They struggled along for many years. The jobs got better and so did the financial struggle. The child grew up, graduated from college, and started her own family. They were not living in luxury, but they were okay. Before they knew it, fifty years had passed. After many struggles, hard times, and unpredictable futures, they were in a good place. They were happy. Yet, he never stopped asking about that cruise.

One night, she had a very vivid dream. In the dream, she was walking down a hallway, and as she walked, she continued to hear, "Book the cruise for him. Book the cruise for him." Normally, when she dreamed, she didn't recall the circumstances of the dream. This time it was perfectly clear. Still, she ignored it. She ignored it until it happened every night for a week. She'd walk down a hallway and would hear the words, "Book the cruise for him."

This concerned her. So she asked him, "Hey, you still want to go on a cruise?"

"You know I do. I've been asking for more than fifty years. Think you can drink that much water?" There was that sly smile that she had come to love so long ago.

So, she booked that cruise. She booked the cruise in April to set sail in December. That way, she could budget and have it all paid for before they ever boarded. She knew when they returned, they would have Christmas and taxes and all the grown-up stuff that senior citizens must do at the end of the year. And it worked. They boarded that ship debt free, and she planned to keep it that way. This was her Christmas gift to him, and her Christmas gift to herself was seeing that sly smile for eight continuous days. Eight glorious days. Key West. Bahamas. The weather was perfect, the sea was calm with the bluest waters they had ever seen, the crew treated them like royalty, and the sights were phenomenal. They had the absolute time of their lives.

During their time on the ship, she kept fighting the constant nagging in the back of her mind to visit the portrait studio. She knew that those photos would be expensive, and she had promised herself that they would leave the ship as debt free as they were when they boarded. But two nights before the end of the cruise, she asked him if he'd like to take photos. They wouldn't have to purchase them. They could just have the experience of doing a photo session on the cruise.

The photos were absolutely beautiful. She couldn't resist buying the entire album. He encouraged it. "Get them," he said. "I don't think you'll regret it."

They docked on a sunny Sunday morning. She drove the four-hour drive back home. As they traveled, they listened to their favorite football team on the radio. Their team was winning. When they arrived home, he went inside first to take care of "personal business" as she pulled the luggage into the kitchen. He'd take it the rest of the way when he joined her in the den. It sure was good to be home. As she waited, she turned on the TV. The football game was still going. Their team was still winning. One of their favorite players made a touchdown. She went to tell him about the remarkable play that the player had just made.

And that's where she found him, collapsed in the hallway, less than an hour after returning home. He was gone, and she was heartbroken. She knew, however, that he left this earth with that sly smile on his face. And he was right. She didn't regret purchasing the beautiful photo album that was still safely packed in the luggage.

The next two months were like she was wandering through a fog, but she was thankful that she had a job to keep her mind busy. It was February 14; Valentine's Day. She entered her workplace and walked to her desk. There, she saw it. A single red rose. No one else knew how it got there. But she did. She knew that he was reminding his valentine that he'd love her forever, and that he was sending it with that sly smile on his face.

# AFTERWORD

By now I expect that you are thinking something like, "After all of the author's research and interviews making this book, does he finally believe in the spirit world on earth?" And the answer is a resounding *yes.* One could discount one report of ghost sightings or two reports or even a dozen reports. But when you have documented over a hundred reports from many various people, decent, average people, people who mostly cannot benefit from lying about experiencing and seeing ghostly apparitions, there has to be something going on here. Most of the eyewitness accounts repeat distinctive commonalities about what other witnesses say, yet the vast majority of these people don't know each other and many of their accounts are separated by large periods of time.

Regarding people not telling the truth: what I have found if anything is that people may lie by their *denying to others that they have seen ghosts when they think they have rather than saying that they have seen ghosts when they haven't.* In general, people only admit to seeing ghosts if their experience was powerful and leaves a lifelong remembrance with them.

We cannot predict or choose when we will be touched by a spiritual event or choose what type. It just happens, usually when we least expect it or want it. It's not like you see in movies and on television. No matter how much one explains what they see and feel and hear to another who hasn't had an experience, one really has to experience the contact themself to truly understand the feeling and what goes on.

I don't think ghosts, for the most part, choose to come into contact with living people. No one really understands their side of the equation. Nonetheless, it is interesting to see who the ghosts do come into contact with and where, when, why, and what they do to and with us.

I would like to invite the reader, if they ever come visit the lovely and historic Central Louisiana, to give me a call. Maybe we can go together and see one or more of these haunted places and maybe, just maybe, we might have the opportunity to meet one of the eternal lost ones.

# BIBLIOGRAPHY

*Major Interviews Conducted by the Author*


Belgard, Kristy
Bergeron Jr., Leon
Bryant, Margaret
Bryant, Tracy
Coco, Phillip
Coen, Cheré Dastugue
Davis, Beulah
Davis, Sylvia Yancy
Farmer, Jan Wilson
Frick, Brenda ("Mimi")
Fritsche, Madylin
Harp Jr., Will
Harper, Celise Reech
Larson, Dr. Jill LeBlanc
Larson, Paul
Laliberte, Scott
McCloud, Felicia
McGimsey, Dr. Chip
McGowen, Cheryl
Owens, Scott
Pillarisetti, Amarjit "Amy"
Pillarisetti, Sudha
Price, Paul
Raines, LeAnn
Rasberry, Douglas
Rasberry, Shirley Bell
Robertson, Dr. Henry
Rodgers, Jen
Ruppert, Brandt
Ruppert, Fane
Ruppert, Gwen
Saunders, Wesley "Wes"
Scarborough, Alice
Swent, Judge Rae D.
Turner, Martha
Tudor, Michael "Mike"
Vandersteen, Beth
Wynne, Michael


*Books and Periodicals*


Barber, Patsy K. *Above the Falls: and Historic Cotile.* Lecompte, Louisiana: Bayou Boeuf Publishing, 1994.

Barber, Patsy K. *Historic Cotile.* Alexandria, Louisiana: Baptist Message Press, 1967.

Branch, Dorothy, et al. *Cheneyville Yesterday: 1812-1980.* Cheneyville, Louisiana: Historic Cheneyville Inc., 1979.

Brister, Elaine H. *Once Upon a River: A History of Pineville, Louisiana.* Baton Rouge, Louisiana: Claitor's Publishing Division, 1968.

Brown, Alan. *Shadows and Cypress: Southern Ghost Stories.* Jackson, Mississippi: University Press of Mississippi, 2000.

Calhoun, Nancy Harris and James Calhoun, Editors. *Plantation Homes of Louisiana.* Gretna, Louisiana: Pelican Publishing Company, 1977.

Coen, Cheré Dastugue. *Haunted Lafayette, Louisiana.* Charleston, South Carolina: The History Press, 2013.

Coleman, Christopher Kiernan. *Dixie Spirits: True Tales of the Strange and Supernatural in the South.* Nashville, Tennessee: Cumberland House Publishing, 2002.

Decuir, Randy P. *Avoyelles Homes: A History of Avoyelles Parish as Seen Through Its Architecture.* Marksville, Louisiana: Gremillion Publishing Company, 1975.

DeHart, Jess. *Plantations of Louisiana.* Gretna, Louisiana: Pelican Publishing Company, 2001.

Dowdy, Verdis H. *Away for a Day in Historical Central Louisiana.* Alexandria, Louisiana: Semple Printing Company, 1977.

DuFour, Darlene. *Kent House: Alexandria, Louisiana.* Pineville, Louisiana: D. D. Management Corporation, 1994.

Duplechien, Brad. *Paranormal Uncensored: A Raw Look at Louisiana Ghost Hunting.* New York: iUniverse, 2008.

Eakin, Sue Lyles and Patsy K. Barber. *Lecompte: Plantation Town in Transition.* Baton Rouge, Louisiana: Venture Productions Inc., 1982.

Eakin, Sue Lyles and Manie Culbertson. *Louisiana: The Land and Its People.* Gretna, Louisiana: Pelican Publishing Company, 1988.

Eakin, Sue Lyles. *Plantations through the Louisiana Heartland Before World War II.* Bossier City, Louisiana: Louisiana State University Agricultural Center, 1988.

Eakin, Sue Lyles. *Rapides Parish: An Illustrated History.* Northridge, California: Windsor Publications Inc., 1987.

Eakin, Sue. *A Sourcebook: Rapides Parish History.* Alexandria, Louisiana: 1976.

Eakin, Sue Lyles. *The Story of Lecompte.* (Private), 1950.

Eskew, Harry G. and Elizabeth. *Alexandria 'Way Down in Dixie: An Informal Biography of An Old Louisiana City.* Alexandria, Louisiana: The Cities of Louisiana Book Series, 1953.

Fonseca, Mary. *Weekend Getaways in Louisiana.* Gretna, Louisiana: Pelican Publishing Company, 1998.

Gremillion, Eleanor. *The History, Services, and Points of Interest in Marksville, Avoyelles Parish.* Marksville, Louisiana: Marksville Chamber of Commerce, 1984.

Hauck, Dennis William. *Haunted Places: The National Directory*. New York: Penguin Books, 2002.

*Historical Survey: Alexandria and Pineville, Louisiana.* Alexandria, Louisiana: Rapides Area Planning Commission, 1973.

Holl, Shelley N. C. *Louisiana Dayride: Fifty-two Short Trips from New Orleans.* Jackson, Mississippi: University Press of Mississippi, 1995.

Hynson, Bobby Downs, Father Chad Partain, and Andrea Wilson Warren. *Under the Shade of the Trees.* Alexandria, Louisiana: Historic Rapides Consulting, 2015.

Jones, Ginger. *Bringing Back the Hotel Bentley.* New Orleans, Louisiana: *Louisiana Cultural Vistas Magazine*, 2015.

Kadlecek, Mabell R. and Marion C. Bullard. *Louisiana's Kisatchie Hills.* Chelsea, Michigan: Book Crafters, 1994.

Kane, Harnett. *Plantation Parade: The Grand Manner in Louisiana.* New York: Bonanza Books, 1945.

Kazek, Kelly. *A Guide to the South's Quirkiest Roadside Attractions.* Charleston, South Carolina: The History Press, 2020.

Laurent, N. B. Carl. *From This Valley: A History of Alexandria, Pineville, and Rapides, Louisiana.* Alexandria, Louisiana: Red River X-Press Historical Publications, 2004.

Laurent, N. B. Carl. *Red River Frontier, Alexandria: 1690-1840.* Alexandria, Louisiana: Red River X-Press Historical Publications, 2003.

Lindahl, Carl, Maida Owens, and C. Renee Harvison. *Swapping Stories: Folktales From Louisiana.* University of Mississippi Press in association with the Louisiana Division of the Arts, 1997.

*Louisiana: A Guide to the State.* New York: Hasting House, 1941.

*Lovely Louisiana.* Baton Rouge, Louisiana: Claude Morgan and Associates, 1956.

Manley, Roger. *Weird Louisiana: Your Travel Guide to Louisiana's Local Legends and Best Kept Secrets.* New York: Sterling Publishing, 2010.

Moran, Mark and Mark Sceurman. *Weird U.S.: Your Travel Guide to America's Local Legends and Best Kept Secrets.* New York: Barnes and Nobles, 2004.

Myers, Arthur. *The Ghostly Register: Haunted Dwellings—Active Spirits, A Journey to America's Strangest Landmarks.* Chicago, Illinois: Contemporary Books Inc., 1986.

Norman, Michael and Beth Scott. *Haunted America.* New York: Tom Doherty Associates, 1994.

Norman, Michael and Beth Scott. *Haunted Heritage.* New York: Tom Doherty Associates, 2002.

Norman, Michael and Beth Scott. *Historic Haunted America.* New York: Tom Doherty Associates, 1995.

O'Bryan, Amis. *Louisiana Ghosts: They Are Among Us.* Sweetwater Press, 2006.

Odom, Keith. *Only In Louisiana: A Guide for the Adventurous Traveler.* Baton Rouge, Louisiana: Quail Ridge Press, 1994.

Pascoe, Jill. *Louisiana's Haunted Plantations.* Baton Rouge, Louisiana: Irongate Press, 2004.

Price, Paul and Michael Wynne. *Old Rapides Cemetery Visitors Guide.* Alexandria, Louisiana: Alexandria-Pineville Area Convention and Visitor's Bureau, 2023.

Saxon, Lyle, Edward Dreyer and Robert Tallant. *Gumbo Ya-Ya.* Gretna, Louisiana: Pelican Publishing Company, 1991.

Saxon, Lyle. *Old Louisiana.* New York: D. Appleton-Century Company, 1929.

Seebold, Herman de Bachelle. *Old Louisiana Plantation Homes and Family Trees.* New Orleans, Louisiana: Pelican Publishing, 1971.

Sillery, Barbara. *Haunted Louisiana.* New Orleans, Louisiana: Pelican Publishing, 2022.

Sillery, Barbara. *The Haunting of Louisiana.* Gretna, Louisiana: Pelican Publishing Company, 2001.

Stafford, George Mason Graham. *General George Mason Graham of Tyrone Plantation and His People.* Baton Rouge, Louisiana: Claitor's Publishing Company, 1981.

Viviano, Christy L. *Haunted Louisiana: True Tales of Ghosts and other Unearthly Creatures.* Metairie, Louisiana: Tree House Press, 1992.

Whittington, G. P. *Rapides Parish Louisiana: A History.* Alexandria, Louisiana: Alexandria Committee of the National Society of the Colonial Dames of America, 1970.

Wlodarski, Robert and Anne Powell Wlodarski. *Southern Friend Spirits: A Guide to Haunted Plantations, Inns, and Taverns.* Plano, Texas: Republic of Texas Press, 2000.

Wood, Christine. *Ghosts Along the Bayou: Tales of Hauntings in Southwestern Louisiana.* Lafayette, Louisiana: Acadiana Press, 1988.

Wynne, Michael. *The Best of Central Louisiana, volumes I, II, III and IV.* Columbia, South Carolina: American History Foundation Publications, 2019-2022.

Wynne, Michael. *Trees Being Lined with Negroes Lynched. . . The True Story of Lynchings in Central Louisiana.* Columbia, South Carolina: American History Foundation Publications, 2022.

Wynne, Michael. *With Burning Zeal. . . The True Story of Lynchings Throughout Central Louisiana.* Columbia, South Carolina: American History Foundation Publications, 2023.

## *Newspapers and Magazines*

Alexandria *Town Talk* newspaper
Alexandria *Cenla Magazine*
Central Louisiana *Cenla Focus* magazine
Marksville *Weekly News* newspaper
Natchitoches *Old Natchitoches Parish Magazine*

## *Television Shows*

*Ghost Hunters,* SyFy Channel
*Haunted Hotels,* Travel Channel
*Haunted Nation,* @hauntednationtv

## *Websites*

Chretien Point, chretienpoint.com
Explore Louisiana, explorelouisiana.com
Ghost 'N' Specters, ghostsnspecters.info
Ghosts of America, ghostsofamerica.com
Louisiana Haunted Houses, louisianahauntedhouses.com
Louisiana Spirits Paranormal, laspirits.com
Roadside America, roadsideamerica.com
Wikipedia

## *Libraries*

Alexandria Genealogical Library, Alexandria, LA
Rapides Parish Library, Alexandria, LA